VIDEOTELLING

YouTube Stories for the Classroom

VIDEO TELLING

YouTube
Stories for the Classroom

Jamie Keddie

Lessonstream
books

All of the videos that provided inspiration for the stories in this book are listed on the accompanying website: www.videotelling.com

When necessary, every reasonable effort has been made to contact the copyright holders for work which inspired the stories in this book. The author is grateful to the following people for granting permission to quote from their videos:
- Alan Melikdjanian ("Captain Disillusion Versus the Tumba Ping Pong Show")
- Alex Overwijk ("World Freehand Circle Drawing Champion")
- Björn Rühmann ("The Wind")
- Joe Tunmer ("Conversation Piece")
- Josh Weiland ("Best Classroom April Fool's Prank Ever")
- Aaron Yonda and Matt Sloan from Blame Society Films ("The Life and Death of a Pumpkin")

ISBN 978 0 9955078 0 7

Credits

Substantive editor: Laura Edlund
Copy editor: Joanna Reid
Illustration: Danny Butcher (dannybutcher.com)
Interior design: Peter Cocking
Cover design: Edward Bettison (edwardbettison.com)
Interior design retouch: Agata Rybicka (agatarybicka.com)
Proofreader: Susie Keddie
Consultancy: Trena White and Megan Jones

To my father Jack - a natural videoteller,
whose enthusiastic descriptions of comedy sketches,
TV moments, film scenes, and viral videos
are usually more entertaining than the real thing.

Contents

Introduction 1

What Is "Videotelling"? 1

Who Is this Book For? 2

How to Use this Book 4

How the Activities Are Organized 4

Preparing for a Videotelling Activity 9

Internal Narratives and the Moment of Comparison 10

How the Book Is Organized 12

1 **Stories from Videos** 14

  1.1 The Visual Narrative 16

  1.2 Transcripts 19

  1.3 Adapting Transcripts 22

  1.4 The Video and You 26

  1.5 The Video and the World 32

  1.6 Combining Narratives 38

2 **Withholding Information** 49

  2.1 The Richard Parker Device 51

  2.2 Witholding Other Facts 56

  2.3 Withholding Genre 59

  2.4 Withholding Outcomes and Endings 62

  2.5 Withholding Incongruity 69

3 **Questioning** *87*
　3.1 Types of Questions *88*
　3.2 The Storyteller's Challenge *104*
　3.3 Students as a Resource *116*
　3.4 Eliciting *121*

4 **Student Interaction Tasks** *133*
　4.1 Questions from Students *134*
　4.2 Isolated Story Items *148*
　4.3 Storytelling Gap Fill *154*
　4.4 Drawing *160*
　4.5 Retelling and Interpreting a Story *165*
　4.6 Designing a Video *170*
　4.7 Collaborative Filmmaking *179*

5 **Media Literacy and Critical Thinking** *185*
　5.1 Sound and Vision *187*
　5.2 Stereotypes and Identity *192*
　5.3 Video Editing *200*
　5.4 Visual Effects *207*
　5.5 Honesty *214*
　5.6 Exploring the Internal Narrative *221*

Appendices *232*
　Appendix 1: Videos, Materials, and Resources *232*
　Appendix 2: Troubleshooting *233*
　Appendix 3: Storytelling Techniques *238*
　Appendix 4: Video Cameras in the Students' Hands *251*
　Appendix 5: Video Cameras in the Teacher's Hands *259*
　Appendix 6: English Language Teachers *266*
　Appendix 7: The "Sneezing Baby Panda" Experiment *273*

About the Author *277*

Acknowledgments *279*

Story Index *280*

My favourite YouTube video ever -
it involves a mother and her baby.

The baby is lying on the floor, sleeping -
dreaming about whatever it is
that babies dream about.

The mother is taking advantage
of this moment of peace.
She is sitting in the corner, eating a snack.

Suddenly, the baby throws out
an incredibly powerful, high-pitched sneeze.

The mother's reaction is absolute comedy ...

She throws up her arms and legs in shock.
She looks down at her baby, as surprised as
we are that something so small
could produce something so loud.

"Sneezing Baby Panda"

Introduced to the world in 2006
Viewed over 250 million times
The most popular animal video on YouTube

....

This book makes many references to many online videos, materials, and other resources. You will find links to all of these on the accompanying website: **www.videotelling.com**

What's this? Find out in appendix 1.

....

Introduction

What Is "Videotelling"?

V*IDEOTELLING* IS A book of interactive stories and activities for teachers to use in their classrooms. Each story is based on the narrative of a short online video and is perfect for engaging "screenagers" and other twenty-first century learners.

The traditional way to use video in the classroom is to watch the video first and talk about it later. The activities in this book reverse that process: Questions, discussion, and analysis come first. A full viewing of the video comes later. This unique approach is what I call "Videotelling".

So how does this work? Well, online videos tend to be short in length but strong in narrative. They present us with perfect, bite-sized stories to share via word of mouth. In a Videotelling activity, the teacher communicates a video narrative through traditional interactive storytelling. In this way, the technology takes a back seat, and human communication comes to the front of the class.

Why storytelling? Storytelling is an age-old pastime with enduring appeal. It is the way we share ideas, explore issues, and build mutual understanding. Through storytelling, we can create a relaxed environment where individuals feel safe to express ideas or simply listen in order to learn from others. For this reason, storytelling can be particularly useful when working with groups of mixed backgrounds and ability.

Through the stories in this book, we can set up activities and tasks for interactive learning and skills development:

- speaking and listening
- discussion and comprehension
- reading and writing
- collaboration between students
- student presentations and storytelling
- video production
- language learning
- media literacy skills
- critical thinking skills

Why online video? Online video is the medium of the moment. On sites like YouTube, young people all over the world are embracing, defining, and constantly reinventing online video. The activities in this book deconstruct viral videos to explore current issues through interactive discussion. They also engage students, get them talking, and encourage passionate, thoughtful communication.

Who Is this Book For?

This book is for many different types of teachers who might be interested in using video and/or storytelling in the classroom:

- English language teachers: For English language learners of all ages (including adults), the immersive story activities in

Videotelling balance intensive listening with conversational skills. Throughout the book, you will find suggestions for teaching grammar and vocabulary. You will also find suggestions for supporting students' comprehension. Look for the "Tips for English Language Teachers" boxes.

- Subject teachers for teens and tweens: Many of the activities in *Videotelling* can be integrated into subject areas such as art, science, mathematics, media studies, film studies, English, and more. Ideas are provided in the "Subject Connections" boxes throughout the book. In addition, the suggested tasks can help students develop and refine their own communication, presentation, and storytelling skills—which apply across subject areas.

- Teachers of primary students: Primary school teachers will be familiar with combining storytelling and visual material. *Videotelling* draws on a bank of short stories, many of which are appropriate for younger classes and will encourage speaking, listening, higher-order thinking, and other capacities.

▶ **Appropriate? Offensive? Safe?**

Many of the stories, videos, and activities in this book will appeal to students of all ages. However, some may include subjects, topics, and language that could be inappropriate, offensive, or unsafe for your students and/or in the context of your teaching environment. In some cases, stories and videos are marked ⓘ to alert you to possible problems. You should always preview videos before showing them to your students; ensure that materials and activities are suitable for your students' age, maturity, and cultural background; and confirm that materials and activities are suitable within the context of your community and school policy. If in doubt, speak with an experienced member of your school's teaching staff.

How to Use this Book

There are various ways to use this book, depending on your teaching and planning style.

1. The cherry picker: Dip in and out of the book at random. Make use of the best-looking stories that you see.
2. The Sunday night lesson planner: Spend some time looking through the chapters to find a story and activity for a specific subject, topic, or language point.
3. The methodologist: Read the book from beginning to end (including appendices). This will provide you with a deeper understanding of the Videotelling approach. I recommend this if you are interested in creating your own Videotelling activities.

How the Activities Are Organized

At the heart of this book, there are forty-five Videotelling activities. Each activity has a three-part layout: the **story**, the **video**, and the **discussion**. Let's have a look at the three parts of an example activity.

Part 1 · Story: "Something Unexpected"

I want to tell you about a very famous video from the early days of YouTube

Perhaps you know it

It involves a mother and her baby

Let's start with the baby[1]

The baby is lying on the floor, sleeping[2]

Meanwhile, the mother is enjoying this moment of peace[3]

She is sitting in the corner, eating a snack

We don't know where the father is[4]

Suddenly, something unexpected happens

As a result, the mother jumps and the baby wakes up[5]

⧖ Part 2 · Video: "Sneezing Baby Panda"

The story "Something Unexpected" is based on a sixteen-second video from the early days of YouTube. It was uploaded in 2006, a year after the birth of the video-sharing site, and is titled "Sneezing Baby Panda". It's currently the most viewed animal video on YouTube and has been copied, parodied, and remixed countless times online.

Part 3 · Discussion

You can turn this story into a whole-class dialogue by pausing to ask the following example questions:

1. *Does anyone in class have a baby or a baby brother or sister? What do you think the baby in the video is doing?*

2. *Do you think that babies dream? What do you think they dream about?*

3. *What about the mother? What do you think she is doing during this peaceful moment?*

4. *Where do you think the father is?*

5. *What do you think happens? Why does the mother jump? Why does the baby wake up?*

After students have shared their ideas, show them the video.

   I have tried this activity with a lot of different students and have demonstrated it to many teachers. Regardless of where I have used it, I am always surprised at how predictable answers tend to be. According to the answers, the mother is usually involved in housework of some kind or another. The father is often at work, on business, or out drinking. Perhaps you could bring this predictability to your students' attention.

▶ **Tips for English Language Teachers**

This activity is good for encouraging students to produce present continuous structures when guessing what the mother and baby are doing. For example:

- *He (the baby) is sleeping, playing with toys, eating, crying, etc.*
- *He is dreaming about his mother or mother's milk, playing with toys, etc.*
- *She (the mother) is checking Facebook, doing the dishes, preparing dinner, etc.*

You can also use the activity to introduce or practise language for speculation. For example:

- *The father could/might be at work, out drinking, on business, etc.*
- *Or maybe/perhaps he's in the kitchen, washing the dishes, preparing dinner, etc.*

▶ **Students as Videotellers**

Ask students to go online and find a funny animal video that they like. They should then prepare a story that describes the video but does not say what the animal or animals are. In order to keep things simple, students can give individual names to the animals and refer to them that way (e.g. Bob, Sarah, Manuel). Later, students can share their stories with each other and try to guess what the mystery animals are in each case. Finally, they should show each other the animal videos that they chose. This can be done in class or online.

About the Stories

All of the stories in the book are contained within boxes. That makes them easy to find. And although they are based on short videos, they have their own titles. For example, the story on page 4 is called "Something Unexpected". But the corresponding video is titled "Sneezing Baby Panda".

The stories deal with a range of topics, and the activities are designed to be interactive in some way or another. For example, in "Something Unexpected", students have to make predictions and also consider whether or not they have seen the video.

Occasionally, the stories may resemble articles, short stories to be read by students, or even recipes. But usually, they are designed to be read aloud. To make this easier for you, they are often shaped like poetry or song lyrics, with one sentence or phrase per line. They may also include other features:

- non-standard punctuation
- subheadings to introduce different story sections
- ellipses (...) to indicate where you should pause or wait for responses
- a numbering system that allows me to refer to certain parts of the story in the discussion (e.g. *Let's start with the baby*[1])
- alternative American English terms provided in brackets. For example, *car park* is followed by (*parking lot*).

As a basic guide for English language teachers, I have graded the stories in appendix 6 according to four levels described by *The Common European Framework of Reference for Languages* (CEFR): elementary (A2), intermediate (B1), upper intermediate (B2), and advanced (C1). In the same appendix, I also provide a list of important words and phrases that appear in each story. This is key language that you may have to introduce to English language learners before they hear the story, for the purpose of comprehension.

You are free to make copies of the stories in this book (scans, photocopies, screen captures, etc.). I would suggest that you create your own notes by writing directly on printed copies of the stories. In addition, you are free to distribute handouts with the stories to your students.

And finally, since I am from the east coast of Scotland, my English may be different from yours. Wherever possible, I have chosen to go with the most internationally recognized language choices, but you should always consider adapting the stories for your own teaching situations and to suit the needs of your students.

About the Video Sections

After each story in the book, you will find a description of the video or videos that the story is based on. All videos can be seen online - usually on YouTube or Vimeo. To find them, you should go to the video site mentioned (usually youtube.com or vimeo. com), type in the name of the video (e.g. "*Sneezing Baby Panda*"), and click *search*. Alternatively, you can find links to all of the videos at **www.videotelling.com**

The videos represent a wide range of genres. They may be short films, incidents caught on camera, music videos, viral videos, advertisements, and much more. The majority of these have come out of online video culture.

You may notice that the story "Something Unexpected" makes no reference to the fact that the protagonists in the corresponding video are pandas. Most of the stories in the book withhold information about the video in some way or another. For students, this can create an element of surprise. Alternatively, it can create a thinking task - a question for students to consider after hearing the story and before seeing the video.

About the Discussions

After each video section, you will find ideas and tips for using the story and video in the classroom:

- suggestions for questions to ask before, during, or after the story (note that there is a numbering system that allows me to refer to specific parts of the story when suggesting questions to ask)

- suggestions for tasks to set before, during, or after the story
- ideas for follow-up activities
- tips for English language teachers (language points to teach, suggestions for supporting student comprehension, etc.)
- suggestions for subject connections (ideas for integrating the stories and activities into curriculum subjects such as art, science, mathematics, film, and media studies)
- other information, such as explanation of concepts or references to other stories

In this section, you will also find ideas for "Students as Videotellers". These provide follow-up suggestions for students to prepare their own Videotelling stories based on online videos. Students can share their stories in one of several ways:

- by telling it live in the classroom (presentation style)
- by handing it in as a written assignment or sharing it in an online space (virtual learning environment, blog, etc.)
- by creating a "talking head" video in which they capture their storytelling performance at home and share the video with the rest of the class. Appendix 4 provides teachers with technical and practical advice for setting up tasks in which students use their own video cameras.

Preparing for a Videotelling Activity

Each activity in this book is arranged so that you can read the story before you watch the video on which it is based. This means that you will be able to experience the stories in the same way as your students will (story first, video second). As you move through this two-step process, consider how students might respond. How might they interpret things and what questions could they ask? There are many things that you can do to prepare for a Videotelling activity:

- Decide whether or not you are going to adapt the story for your students' needs.
- Familiarize yourself with the story and practise reading it aloud from the page or from memory if you prefer.
- Decide what storytelling devices you are going to use. You will find many suggestions for these in appendix 3 – use of gesture, repetition, space, etc.
- Make notes to use in class. Notes should provide you with essential information about what you are going to say, what you are going to ask, or what grammar or vocabulary you are going to teach. They can take the form of a set of cue cards, a flow diagram, a mind map, or a list of bullet points. Alternatively, you can photocopy the stories from this book and write your own notes over the top of them.
- Make copies of the story to distribute to your students. You may decide that some stories work better for activities that involve reading. In addition, English language learners will often appreciate a copy of the story text for their own reference.
- Make any changes to the classroom seating arrangement. For interactive storytelling, a circle or a horseshoe formation works well.
- Decide how you will let students see the video (display it on a projector in class, give students instructions to find it online and watch it later, etc.).

Internal Narratives and the Moment of Comparison

Consider the activities that take place in our minds when we watch a video or listen to a story. We deconstruct plots and storylines. We judge protagonists and evaluate their decisions. We form opinions and draw conclusions. We ask questions and speculate about answers. In short, we create our own narratives.

Although we may all see the same video, read the same book, or listen to the same news report, we will all respond to the experience in a different way. In this book, I use the term "internal narrative" to refer to an individual's experience of a story or video.

In addition, the stories in this book make use of a universal resource, one that can easily be forgotten in this image-saturated world: the mind's eye (or perhaps, mind's computer screen!). Of course, there is nothing new about visualization activities, but there is something that makes the stories in this book different: After listening to them, students get the opportunity to see the corresponding videos. This experience gives students the chance to compare the mental images that they constructed with the ones they see on the screen.

Throughout this book, I will refer to this opportunity as "the moment of comparison". The moment of comparison can be compared with the familiar process of seeing a dramatization of a book that you have already read. The moment of comparison can be a moment of realization, impact, and learning. It is the time when confusion is resolved, questions are answered, and comprehension is strengthened.

However, a word of advice to teachers: Before the moment of comparison, try to forget that there is a video coming. When telling a story, focus on the thoughts and ideas that your students offer. Worry less about what is right and what is wrong. In other words, the internal narratives that students create in response to a story are more important than the video. This is a book about negotiating, not dictating, video narratives.

After the Moment of Comparison

Once students have heard a story and seen the video, an activity can be taken in many directions, and I offer various suggestions throughout the book. However, one less obvious but beneficial direction is backwards – to revisit the story after watching the video.

The reason for this is simple – the video can strengthen students' comprehension of the story text. For example, the story "Something Unexpected" contains the line: "As a result, the mother jumps and the baby wakes up." There are many ways in which students could miscomprehend this. They might imagine that the baby wakes up because the mother jumps (a cause and effect issue). Or they may take the image literally and imagine the mother leaving the ground. Fortunately, the video will clarify confusion like this.

By revisiting the story text after watching the video, students may notice or appreciate things that they didn't get the first time around. This approach can be especially important for learners of English, who will get an extra opportunity to meet the language of the story one more time.

When revisiting the story, English language teachers can draw their learners' attention to specific words, phrases, or grammar choices in the text by creating gap fills or other language study exercises. In the following example, students have to choose the correct form of the verb:

- *The video **involves/is involving** a mother and her baby.*
- *The baby **lies/is lying** on the floor, sleeping.*
- *Meanwhile, the mother **enjoys/is enjoying** this moment of peace.*
- *She **sits/is sitting** in the corner, eating a snack.*
- *We don't know where the father is. Perhaps he **prepares/is preparing** the dinner.*
- *Suddenly, something unexpected **happens/is happening**. As a result, the mother **jumps/is jumping** and the baby **wakes up/ is waking up**.*

How the Book Is Organized

This book consists of forty-five Videotelling activities organized into five chapters, followed by appendices. Throughout the book, you will find headings that will help you skim the contents and find activities, ideas, tips, suggestions, examples, options, and follow-ups.

Each chapter has a different focus, and to an extent, the chapters build on each other. This means that you will benefit from a deeper understanding of the Videotelling approach if you start at the beginning and read to the end. The chapters are as follows:

- •"Chapter 1: Stories from Videos" deconstructs videos and explores possibilities for creating stories from them.

- •"Chapter 2: Withholding Information" focuses on the different types of information in a video that we can choose to strategically exclude from the story.

- •"Chapter 3: Questioning" focuses on asking questions and responding to students' answers when storytelling.

- •"Chapter 4: Student Interaction Tasks" explores the many ways that we can make stories interactive and get students involved.

- •"Chapter 5: Media Literacy and Critical Thinking" digs deeper into online video and addresses issues related to how the videos are made (such as the use of sound, production, and editing techniques), and also explores questions related to bias and how the world is represented (e.g. stereotyping).

The appendices provide support for all chapters. They offer a complementary collection of practical and technical ideas, strategies, and suggestions.

The stories and video names are also included in indexes at the end of the book so that you can access them in various ways.

Well, now it's time for the main course: the stories, the videos, and the activities. I hope you enjoy them as much as your students will.

Happy Videotelling!

Jamie :)

◀ 1 ▶

Stories from Videos

I SPEND A LOT of time on video-sharing sites – too much, some would say! I am always looking for a new video for my next story. For me, the perfect video is short in length but rich in narrative. As well as providing an engaging viewing experience, it will feed the imagination.

Narratives can extend beyond the rectangular window on your computer screen. Once we start to investigate the *who*, *what*, *when*, *where*, *why*, and *how* that relate to a video, a story can start to go in many different directions.

This chapter introduces some different starting points for creating video-based stories. We will see that there are three different levels that can be explored:

1. The video itself: A basic description of what you see and what you hear in the video.

2. You, the viewer: An exploration of the activity that takes place in your own mind in response to the video – for example, the

questions that you ask and the answers that your imagination supplies. In this book, this is referred to as the internal narrative.

3. The world: Investigation into the video – the story behind it. Sometimes, the most fundamental questions to ask are: *Who created the video, why, and how?*

 All videos, materials, and resources mentioned in this chapter can be accessed at **www.videotelling.com** For more information, see appendix 1.

Creating Your Own Video-Based Stories

Creating a video-based story requires a lot of viewing, thinking, investigating, writing, experimenting, reflecting, and rewriting. As a process, this is a very personal one. If you were to create a story based on one of the videos in this book, the structure, details, and language choices would be completely different from mine.

This book is designed so that you will experience the story first and the video second. However, if you are interested in creating your own stories from video, you could reverse that process: watch the video first, consider how you would base a story on it, and then compare your story with mine.

1.1 The Visual Narrative

"The visual narrative" is the story that the moving images tell. Most of the stories in this book have a very strong connection with visual narratives. Virtually all of them make reference to the people, the objects, the locations, the events, and the actions that we see in videos.

The following story is based on the visual narrative of a short video that was filmed at a zoo.

Story: "Feeding Time"

It's feeding time and Boris and Amba are hungry
On the menu today we have watermelons – whole watermelons!

Boris goes first
He stands with his mouth wide open
Waiting patiently

The zookeeper picks up a watermelon
And drops it into his mouth

Boris closes his mouth and . . .
You can actually see and hear the watermelon burst
He raises his head so that the juice runs down his throat

Now it's Amba's turn
She stands with her mouth wide open
Waiting patiently

The zookeeper picks up another watermelon
And drops it into her mouth

Amba closes her mouth
She crushes the fruit as if it were a grape
She raises her head so that the juice runs down her throat

▶

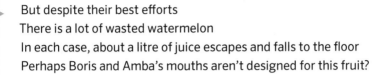

> But despite their best efforts
> There is a lot of wasted watermelon
> In each case, about a litre of juice escapes and falls to the floor
> Perhaps Boris and Amba's mouths aren't designed for this fruit?

Video: "Hippos Eating Whole Watermelons"

On YouTube, there are many videos of hippos being fed whole watermelons. Most were filmed at Nagasaki Bio Park in Japan and the best one is on their official YouTube channel. It shows two hungry hippos in the same enclosure. The video's Japanese title translates as "Hippos Whole Watermelon Time". As with all of the videos mentioned in this book, you can access this one directly from the accompanying resource webpage (see appendix 1 for the link and details).

Discussion

While you tell this story, pause and invite students to guess what kind of animals Boris and Amba might be. Common answers include elephants, crocodiles, sharks, and bears.

► Subject Connections

Science teachers could use this story to introduce the subject of animals' diets. Hippopotamuses and elephants are herbivorous. Crocodiles and most sharks are carnivorous. Bears are omnivorous.

► Tips for English Language Teachers

You can use this story to introduce nouns that can exist in countable or uncountable forms. Watermelon is a perfect example. Ask students if it would be more usual to ask someone: *Do you like watermelon?* or *Do you like watermelons?* The first question sounds more natural. Since humans don't usually eat whole watermelons, it is normal for us to use the uncountable form of this noun when talking about food (*I like apples and watermelon.*; *a bowl of watermelon*; *Watermelon is my favourite fruit.*). Hippos are different. If they could talk, they might say: "We like watermelons."

▶ **Students as Videotellers**

Ask students to go online and find a video in which an animal is eating or being fed. They should then write a description of the video without saying what the animal or food is. In order to do this, they can give the animal a name or they can refer to the mystery meal. Later, students can share their stories and in each case guess what the mystery animals or meals are.

1.2 Transcripts

Sometimes, when a video contains spoken words (a monologue or a dialogue), we can transcribe the words and make use of the text. When presented with an isolated transcript, students can neither hear nor see the speaker. They will have to use their imaginations to provide this missing information.

The following story is the transcript of a video:

Story: "Always Misunderstood" ⓘ

I think I was always misunderstood
People just didn't seem to like me
I think I annoyed them
I got on their nerves
I don't know why
That's just the way it was
Maybe I was too intense
Maybe I came on too strong
I don't know — I really can't say
Yeah, it was lonely, really lonely
But you get used to it after a while
And then one day, everything changed
Somebody finally accepted me for what I am
Since I got this job, life has been completely different
I finally feel useful — good at something

Video: "Epuron – The Wind" (or "Mr. W")

This text is taken from a 2007 advertisement, which was a collaboration between an energy company called Epuron and the German Ministry for the Environment. The advert features a mystery man with a French accent. He speaks to the camera and tells us his life story. His words are accompanied by sad piano music and intercut with footage of the annoying things that he used to do: dropping flower pots from balconies, knocking people's hats off, throwing sand at children in playgrounds, turning umbrellas inside out.

The "Mr. W" video has a strong audio narrative. As well as the music, it contains background sounds that reinforce the actions shown in the video (a woman's scream, footsteps, the smashing of a flower pot, etc.).

At the end of the advertisement, we learn that the man's new job is turning the blades of wind turbines. We realize that this character is not a man at all, but rather a personification of the wind.

The advertisement was directed by Björn Rühmann and won a number of awards, including a Cannes Gold Lion. Its original title was "Epuron - The Wind". But on the internet, the advertisement is better known by its unofficial title: "Mr. W".

Discussion

One standard way of using video in the classroom is to take an audio-only approach. A typical audio-only activity might work like this: The teacher plays a video so that students can hear it but not see it. Students then answer questions and do other tasks that require them to listen and use their imaginations. For example, they consider: What is happening here? How many people are speaking, and where are they? After students compare their ideas, the teacher shows the video.

In the case of the "Mr. W" advertisement, an audio-only approach would allow students to hear the man's French accent, the sad piano music, and background sound effects. All of these things would influence the images that students create in their mind's eye.

However, when you read the "Always Misunderstood" story, you were denied all of this information. You didn't even know if the words belonged to a man or a woman. The story could be anybody's. It becomes more open-ended. The story deals with emotions and issues that are universal: loneliness, rejection, and acceptance. Its simplicity also adds to its appeal: it starts with a problem and ends with a resolution.

Without the audio track or visual of the video, the story based on the transcribed words alone becomes stripped of context. We create our own meaning by asking questions and guessing answers. The stories and activities in this book exploit ambiguity in this way.

When using the story "Always Misunderstood" in class, don't tell students its source. Read the story and ask students to note the questions that occur to them as they listen. Read it two or three times, and in each case write all suggested questions on the board. These may be questions about the character and narrative:

- *Whose words are these?*
- *What is the person's name?*
- *What did the person do to annoy people or get on people's nerves?*
- *Why did he or she do those things?*
- *Where is he or she from?*
- *Who finally accepted him or her?*
- *What is his or her new job?*

It's important that you do not supply answers to these questions. That is the students' job. As is the case with all of the stories in this book, the students' imaginations are more important than the facts of the video; internal narratives are at the heart of the activity.

Ask students to use their imaginations and invent answers to these questions. They can do this on their own, in pairs, or in small groups. By answering the questions, students will construct a narrative of their own that tells the story of the mystery character. Perhaps it will be subliminally autobiographical.

Students can use these stories for the basis of their own invented stories. It can be interesting to hear students' ideas of annoying habits that can be harnessed constructively. Stories from my own students have involved individuals finding jobs in life as football referees, traffic police, and even teachers!

After students have had time to create and share their own narratives, tell them that you also have a story. At this point, show them the video.

▶ **Subject Connections**

You might want to use the story and video to explore renewable energy sources and environmental studies. For teachers of media and film studies, the video is perfect for illustrating an editing technique which indicates flashbacks. Additional footage, which is referred to as B-roll, is intercut with the main shot. In this case, the B-roll shows the things that Mr. W did to get on people's nerves.

1.3 Adapting Transcripts

The previous story consisted of a short monologue – the transcribed words of a mystery character called Mr. W. But if you compare the words in the story text with the actual words in the video, you will notice that I made a minor change:

- *Since I've got this job, life is completely different.* (These are Mr. W's actual words in the video.)

- *Since I got this job, life has been completely different.* (These are the words as they appear in my story text.)

So why did I make this change? Well, Mr. W breaks a grammar rule that students of English are expected to follow in examinations. As a teacher of English, I want to provide my students with samples of language that they are expected to produce in such situations. Of course, your situation may be different, and you may wish to leave the original words.

Although my change might seem insignificant, I mention it to illustrate a point: Teachers can adapt language to suit the needs of their students and the requirements of a course. Here are some other possible reasons for adapting transcripts of spoken words in videos:

- The transcript is too long. In this case, you might want to shorten it, use an excerpt, or remove a part.

- The transcript contains cultural references or ideas that unnecessarily complicate matters for the students.

- The transcript contains low-frequency words, phrases, idioms, or structures. For the purpose of comprehension, you can replace these with language that is more common and easily understood by the students.

- The transcript contains non-standard or maverick language that breaks the rules that you are obliged to work with. You can change the language accordingly.

In my experience, students rarely notice the discrepancy between an adapted transcript and the exact words that they hear in the video. But if they do spot differences, my advice is to be honest – admit that you made some changes and give your reasons for doing so.

The following is another video transcript which I have adapted. If a reader does not know anything about the video, the original transcript can seem quite violent and may give some students nightmares. For this reason, I have changed some of the language to make it less graphic. I have also shortened the text and simplified it for learners of English. Finally, I have reworked parts of the text in order to make it easier to read aloud.

Story: "Halloween Horror Story" ⊡

In the beginning, my life was peaceful
Days spent with my family in the garden
The sunlight warming my skin
Peaceful

And then one day, they came without warning
Cruel hands dragging me from my dreams
Into a wheeled box

They carried me past my brothers and sisters, my friends and family
I cried for help but my kin remained silent
My home began to fade in the distance
And suddenly
Everything went dark

When I woke up, I found myself on hard grey earth
Where was I?
And then they came
With large kitchen knives!

The pain was terrible — I became dizzy — I felt sick
They made a giant hole in my head
They pulled my insides out and threw them in front of me
Like ribbons from a gift

When they finished, I sat in shock
Praying that it was over
But of course . . .
It was not!
The knives returned
They cut a face in my side
And they put a stick of hot fire in my belly
Burning, burning flame!

Who were these people and why did they do this to me?
Why? Why? Why?

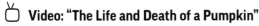 **Video: "The Life and Death of a Pumpkin"**

In this short comedy film, we meet an unfortunate pumpkin who is picked from the field, taken home, and turned into a jack-o'-lantern at Halloween. The film "The Life and Death of a Pumpkin" was directed by Aaron Yonda and won the Best Short Film and Best Concept awards at the 2006 Chicago Horror Film Festival. Voice actor Matt Sloan provides a great voiceover for the pumpkin.

Discussion

Some people might find this story quite shocking, especially before they realize that the protagonist is a pumpkin. Be aware of this possibility and be sympathetic to your students.

Before telling the story, write the following phrases on the board and tell students that all these items feature in a horror story:

- *a wheeled box*
- *hard grey earth*
- *a stick of hot fire*
- *a face in my side*

Ask students to speculate about what the phrases could refer to and ask them to guess what happens in the story.

Before reading the story, reassure students that although it might sound horrific, they will discover that it is not all that bad. You could even tell them from the beginning that the words do not belong to a human or animal, and ask them to guess what the object is.

Read the story two or three times. Pause when you get to each of the four phrases on the board and again ask students to consider what they could be describing. Also, ask students to guess who or what the character is, and what it looks like.

After you have encouraged students to make some guesses, show them the short film. They should be able to attach meaning to key phrases:

- *a wheeled box* is a wheelbarrow
- *hard grey earth* is the pavement
- *a stick of hot fire* is a candle
- *a face in my side* is a face carved in the jack-o'-lantern

---

▶ **Subject Connections**

For teachers of history, you could use this story to set up a project in which students investigate and explore the origin of Halloween.

▶ **Students as Storytellers**

Ask students to write their own horror stories based on the lives and deaths of food items or everyday objects. They could choose to talk about strawberries being made into jam, a golf ball being hit by a golf club, or a dog's toy being chewed to death. Students should write in the first person. Later, invite students to share their stories and have others guess what the mystery objects or food items are.

▶ **Tips for English Language Teachers**

For learners of English, you may wish to point out the following play on words: *I cried for help but my kin remained silent.* In this sense, *kin* has two meanings: family members and also a shortened version of the word *pumpkin* (not standard).

1.4 The Video and You

Creating story texts is a personal process. We have to decide what to include in the story and how to put it into words. These decisions will depend on the details that we notice in the video and our own personal language choices.

We can go even further than that and explore our internal narrative - the story that we construct in our own minds in response to the video. This, in itself, is a valuable resource. As you watch a video, become aware of your own mental processes:

- missing information and details that your imagination provides
- questions and other thoughts that form in your mind (for example, ideas about what happened before or after the video was created)
- memories or past experiences that you recall
- your opinions of the people in the video and those who created it
- personal interpretations, analyses, criticisms, and judgments

The following stories have come out of my own imagination in response to two viral videos that I like.

Story: "Eagle Eyes"

Elizabeth didn't wear glasses
Why would she?
She had perfect eyesight

Elizabeth didn't wear contact lenses
Why would she?
She could see perfectly

Elizabeth didn't need binoculars
Why would she?
She had eagle eyes

One day, Elizabeth was sitting on her favourite branch
In her favourite tree
When suddenly
In the distance
She spotted something
That would change her life . . .
Forever!

What did Elizabeth see and how did it change her life?

📺 Video: "Dramatic Eagle"

This story is based on a viral video titled "Dramatic Eagle". In the video, an eagle is being filmed with a telephoto lens. Suddenly, the eagle turns around, looks directly at the camera, and opens its beak wide. As it does so, the camera zooms in. The five-second event is accompanied by three dramatic chords, which sound as if they could have been borrowed from an old kung fu movie.

"Dramatic Eagle" is a parody of another viral video from the early days of YouTube, "Dramatic Chipmunk". You can read more about the "Dramatic Chipmunk" meme on Wikipedia — appendix 1 provides instructions for finding links that are referred to throughout the book.

Discussion

After reading the story, show the video and ask students to create a short story about what Elizabeth saw and how it changed her life.

Of course, the question is open-ended. We cannot know why Elizabeth reacted the way she did, but students might be interested to know the context of the video. You can refer them to the original video "Dramatic Chipmunk" as well as to some of the other parodies ("Dramatic Dog", "Dramatic Cat", etc.). As mentioned above, there is also a Wikipedia page which explains this meme.

▶ **Subject Connections**

Many stories and videos in *Videotelling* present the opportunity to explore with students *viral videos, memes, parody videos, satire, humour, mashups,* and other terms that relate to media studies, communication studies, English, and the arts.

Story: "An Act of True Love" (!)

1. Obsessed
Manuel loved Isabel
She was the love of his life
Manuel was crazy about her
Absolutely obsessed with her
She was all he had ever wanted
All he had ever dreamed about
Manuel spent every moment of the day thinking about her

Isabel never complained
Why would she?
Manuel treated her well — He looked after her — He took care of her
He took her out almost every night
He spent time with her
He spent money on her

▶

2. Hail

According to Wikipedia
The largest recorded hailstone
Was 20 centimetres in diameter
That's as big as a melon
You wouldn't want that to land on your head

Fortunately, on the day that Manuel left Isabel under a tree
The hailstones that fell from the sky
Were much smaller than melons
They were probably about the size of grapes
Nevertheless, a frozen grape —
If dropped on your head from a height — could hurt

3. Courage

Manuel looked back at Isabel
His first thought was that the tree would protect her
But it did no such thing
The hailstones passed through the leaves and branches like bullets

Without any concern for his own safety
Manuel ran back to Isabel as fast as he could
And like a true hero, he threw himself on top of her
Desperate to shield her from the danger

Now, unfortunately, Isabel was considerably larger than Manuel
And as a result, Manuel was unable to cover her completely
And although most of the hailstones bounced off Manuel's back
Much of Isabel was left exposed

Determined not to let another single hailstone make contact with her body
Manuel reacted instinctively:
He started to make furious movements with his arms and legs
Hoping that the more he moved, the more he would protect her

4. Raphael

Above the tree, Raphael stood at his window
He was smiling devilishly with his video camera in his hand
He was pointing it at the scene below:
His eccentric neighbour Manuel, on top of his precious Isabel
Flapping his arms and flapping his legs
Like a man being attacked by bees
Or frozen grapes
Raphael thought to himself: *This is definitely going on YouTube*

Video: "Man Desperately Tries to Protect His Car from Hail"

This story is based on a video that has been uploaded onto virtually every video-sharing site that I can name. At least twelve different people have uploaded it onto YouTube. I have no idea where or when it was filmed. Nor do I know who filmed it, who uploaded it, or who owns it. Since there are multiple copies of the video online, there are many different titles. But the one that I feel captures it best is "Man Desperately Tries to Protect His Car from Hail".

Discussion

I was going to suggest that, before showing students the video, you ask them to draw the scene as they imagine it would appear through Raphael's video camera. But this might be a bad idea – I can imagine a lot of you holding me responsible for students' inappropriate illustrations!

Perhaps you could use this as a Friday afternoon story. Just before students leave for the weekend, tell them the story, show them the video, and let them leave with a smile on their faces.

▶ **Students as Videotellers**

One option for extending the activity is to follow it with a creative writing task. Tell students that they are going to create a similar story of their own, which should also be based on a short online video.

Students can choose their own videos or you can suggest one yourself. A good choice would be "Just Call the Police, Baby". From the inside of her car, a woman films a pickup truck overtaking her on the highway. Lying on the hood of the truck is a man. As he passes, he looks up at the woman and pleads for her to call the police. When she inquires what's going on, he replies nonchalantly: "Just call the police, baby." This twenty-two-second video went viral on YouTube in 2013.

1.5 The Video and the World

Sometimes we can step away from the video itself and consider the bigger picture. We can ask ourselves who created it and why. We can find out about the tools and techniques that they used. We can investigate background facts and events. In short, we can look for stories *about* videos.

In the internet age, anyone with a smartphone can create and share a video. And anyone with online access can interact. As a result, a video can come from anywhere and find itself in a complex and constantly changing web of narratives. This unpredictability has always made the internet an excellent source of material for storytellers.

This also means that every online video is an artifact. And in order to investigate the external narratives for an artifact, students will have to investigate the *who, what, when, where, why,* and *how* questions that relate to it:

- *Who created the video and why?*
- *Where and when was it created?*
- *What equipment, tools, and techniques were involved?*
- *When was it uploaded? On what video-sharing sites was it uploaded?*
- *How many times has it been viewed?*
- *Is there any historical or cultural information that we need in order to appreciate it?*
- *Is it associated with any other videos? For example, is it part of a series?*
- *How do or did people interact with it?*
- *If a video went viral, how did this happen?*
- *Are there any spoofs, spinoffs, or parodies of the video?*

Sometimes, a popular story that is born on social media will be reported by the mainstream media. As a result, the story can then take different directions. And of course, any prominent viral video will leave behind a stream of copy, parody, and remix videos. The following story shows just how unpredictable and fascinating the world of online video can get.

Story: "A Tale of Two Ryans"

It's incredible how much you can say in just six seconds.

On May 5, 2015, a man uploaded a six-second video. The video starts with a close-up shot of a bowl of cornflakes. After adding milk, the man takes a spoonful of the cereal, holds it up to the camera, and then confidently puts it in his mouth.

Within days, the video was viewed millions of times. Why?[1]

The story begins two years earlier. In April 2013, the same man started to appear in a series of six-second online videos. But in each of those videos, he refused to eat his cereal.[2]

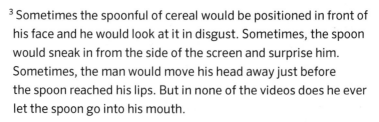

[3] Sometimes the spoonful of cereal would be positioned in front of his face and he would look at it in disgust. Sometimes, the spoon would sneak in from the side of the screen and surprise him. Sometimes, the man would move his head away just before the spoon reached his lips. But in none of the videos does he ever let the spoon go into his mouth.

The man would never smile. He often looked serious, as if he was lost in thought. Perhaps he was nervous or upset about something. It was always difficult to tell.

The series consisted of over thirty videos and ran for two years.[4,5] It was created by a young Scottish director called Ryan McHenry. The man who refused to eat his cereal was Hollywood actor Ryan Gosling.[6]

Ryan McHenry created his videos by directly filming his TV screen while physically holding a spoonful of cereal in front of it. The images on the screen would be carefully chosen moments from Ryan Gosling films: dialogue-free, close-up shots of the actor.

Out of context, we could never be sure what was going on in the films. But in each of Ryan McHenry's videos, the storyline would seem to involve the spoonful of cereal.

The series received a lot of attention on social and mainstream media. Many people seemed to find the idea both silly and ingenious.[7]

Sadly, on May 2, 2015, Ryan McHenry died from bone cancer.[8] Three days later, Ryan Gosling uploaded his tribute video – a cereal salute from one Ryan to another.

It's incredible how much you can say in just six seconds.[9]

⌣ Videos: The "Ryan Gosling Won't Eat His Cereal" Series and Ryan Gosling's Response

The videos in this story were shared on the video platform Vine. The most notable thing about Vine videos is that they have to be six seconds long. This restriction has led to some quite interesting and creative online cultures. The "Ryan Gosling Won't Eat His Cereal" videos can be seen on Ryan McHenry's Vine channel as well as his YouTube channel.

On May 5, 2015, Ryan Gosling created his own Vine channel and uploaded his video tribute to Ryan McHenry. Within days, the video went to the top of Reddit and was viewed millions of times. Reddit is a website where community members share content that they find on the internet. Content is then voted up or down by other users.

Remember that you will find links to all of these videos on the accompanying website - see appendix 1 for information.

Discussion

In the classroom, I would suggest telling the story "A Tale of Two Ryans", showing some of the videos and asking questions as you do so:

1. *Why do you think a six-second video of a man eating cereal could be so popular?*

2. *Can anyone make sense of this story so far?*

3. *Let me describe the videos for you. Now please listen carefully – I want you to imagine how they appear.*

4. *The videos appeared on a video platform called Vine. Does anyone know about Vine?*

5. Show students a selection of the videos from the "Ryan Gosling Won't Eat His Cereal" series and ask: *Has anyone seen these videos before? Do you know who Ryan Gosling is? Who created these videos and why?*

6. *Can you guess how Ryan McHenry made the videos?*

7. *Why do you think the videos were so popular? What do you think of them? Would you describe them as either silly or ingenious? Why?*

8. *When Ryan McHenry passed away, can you guess what Ryan Gosling did?* (note that this will take students back to the beginning of the story)

9. *Is there anything that we can learn from this story? Can you think of any other stories in which someone's life changed as a result of something that happened on the internet?*

"A Tale of Two Ryans" can be regarded as a case study – a look at the diversity of viral video stories and video cultures that emerge online. For homework, you could ask your students to investigate and document a story that has an online video at its heart. If students are stuck for an example, give them some suggestions. Below you will find a list of stories that involve online videos. In order to appreciate these stories, students will need to research them. In other words, they will have to investigate the external narratives:

- Free Hugs Campaign (2006)
- Rickrolling (from 2007)
- Techno Viking (2007)
- Keyboard Cat (2009)
- Fenton the Dog in Richmond Park (2011)
- Nyan Cat (2011)
- "Hey You! What Song Are You Listening To?" (2011)
- The Harlem Shake (2013)
- The Stoner Sloth Anti-Marijuana Campaign (2015)
- Duck Army (2015)
- Reddit Revives Ninety-Three-Year-Old Pianist Wally Kraus (2015)

In some cases, Wikipedia can be a good place to investigate stories about videos. All of the following are entries that refer specifically to viral videos:

- Everyday (video)
- Boom Goes the Dynamite
- The Bus Uncle
- Chocolate Rain
- Dramatic Chipmunk
- Charlie Bit My Finger
- Battle at Kruger
- David after Dentist
- JK Wedding Entrance Dance
- United Breaks Guitars
- Double Rainbow (viral video)
- Ain't Nobody Got Time for That
- Chewbacca Mask Lady

▶ **Subject Connections**

This story has obvious connections to media studies. For teachers of literature and film studies, "A Tale of Two Ryans" could be used to demonstrate nonlinear or non-chronological story structure. The story begins at the end – the moment when Ryan Gosling uploads his video tribute to Ryan McHenry. Out of context, this key event both confuses and intrigues the listener or reader. Later, as things develop, everything makes sense. This is a fundamental technique which is used in literature, screenwriting, documentary writing, and storytelling in general.

1.6 Combining Narratives

In this chapter, we have considered the three levels that we can work with when creating story texts from video:

1. what we see and hear (the video itself)
2. what we think and imagine in response (the internal narrative)
3. what we know or discover about the video (external narratives)

Inevitably, any story text can operate on all three levels. To demonstrate this, consider the following story:

Story: A "World Champion"

It's ten o'clock in the morning. The video camera is turned on and pointed at Alex. The image is shaky.

"Why don't you tell us the story?"

"I'm going to tell you the story", says Alex as he cleans the board with a wet sponge. "This is something that I used to do in my spare time. Then one day I discovered that there is an annual world championship held in Las Vegas. Now, as a previous winner, I automatically get invited back every year."

Alex prepares to demonstrate his talent. He warms up by doing a special exercise with his right arm. Alex is tall and thin – perhaps the ideal build for doing what he does. He is wearing loose clothes. Perfect. He doesn't want to restrict his upper body. Perhaps he came to work prepared?

The board is still wet. Alex attempts to make it dry faster by flapping his hands at it comically. This seems to entertain his audience. It makes them laugh.

Alex picks up a piece of chalk. He takes a deep breath and stands tall beside the board. He is focused and ready. His audience is silent.

▶

And then . . .

The movement is perfect. The audience applauds. The video finds its way onto YouTube and goes viral. Alex becomes famous on the internet.

Video: "World Freehand Circle Drawing Champion"

In this video, Canadian mathematics teacher Alexander Overwijk tells his students that he is the world champion at drawing freehand circles. He then demonstrates his skill by drawing a perfect circle on the blackboard. The video was filmed by one of his students. It was uploaded onto YouTube in 2007 and is titled "World Freehand Circle Drawing Champion".

As a teacher who loves to tell stories in the classroom, I always wondered if Alex was being completely honest with his students. Is he really the world freehand circle drawing champion? Or is this a little white lie? I once had the pleasure of meeting Alex and was able to ask him this very question. He told me the truth behind his video but made me promise that I wouldn't tell anyone!

Discussion

In writing this story, I made use of the following:

- The visual narrative: I referred to the people, objects, and actions in the video – the things that we see (Alex, the blackboard, the warm-up exercise, etc.).

- Spoken language: I referred to the things that people said but I did so selectively. I chose those utterances which I felt were most important to the story. And I adapted them when I felt it necessary.

- Non-verbal aspects of the audio: The story makes reference to laughter, silence, and applause.

- The external narrative: I had to investigate the story behind the video to get the teacher's name. I also mention that the video goes viral on YouTube and this results in internet fame for Alex.

- My internal narrative: Different people notice different things in the same video. And when different people see similar things, they use different language to describe them. A lot of my story contains speculation. For example, I suggest that Alex's physical build is ideal for drawing freehand circles and suggest that he came to work prepared. There is also interpretation - the use of the word *comically*, for example.

In the classroom, before you tell students the story "A World Champion", write the following questions on the board:

- *Where do you think this exchange takes place?*
- *What do you think Alex does for a living?*
- *Who do you think his audience is? What is his relationship with them?*
- *What do you think his special talent is?*

Tell the story two or three times. Each time you reach the end of the story, ask students to speculate and elaborate on their answers. You can also encourage students to make sense of the story by asking you questions.

After students have shared their ideas, show them the video. As a follow-up, ask students whether they think that Alex is being truthful with his students. Ask them to watch the video carefully, make a decision, and give reasons for their answers. Students can then go online to check the facts of Alex's story. When they do so, it is possible that they will make some interesting discoveries. I have included some links on the accompanying website - see appendix 1 for access instructions.

▶ **Tips for English Language Teachers**

In order to make the story simpler and more understandable for your students, adapt the story text and/or prepare the students as necessary. For example, you could tell students from the start that Alex is a teacher demonstrating a special talent to his students.

The story contains a lot of adjectives (see the bold words in the list of phrases below). Before you tell the story, write the list below on the board and invite students to guess what happens. When you tell the story a second or third time, pause when you arrive at each of the adjectives and invite students to recall it.

- *a **shaky** image*
- *a **wet** sponge*
- ***spare** time*
- *an **annual** world championship*
- *a **previous** winner*
- *a **special** exercise*
- *his **right** arm*
- ***tall** and **thin***
- *the **ideal** build*
- ***loose** clothes*
- *his **upper** body*
- *a **deep** breath*
- ***focused** and **ready***
- *a **silent** audience*
- *a **perfect** movement*
- *a **viral** video*
- ***famous** on the internet*

▶ **Subject Connections**

Teachers of mathematics could use the story and video as an opportunity to introduce the topic of circles. Art and art history teachers could follow up with stories and instances of circles in art. For example, Rembrandt's *Self Portrait with Two Circles* contains fragments of two circles in the background of the painting. Ask students to go online for homework and investigate the various theories about the circles. One theory is that they symbolize the perfection of Rembrandt's artistic skill; other theories suggest that they refer to the story of Giotto, the Italian master who — when summoned by the Pope to demonstrate his artistry — responded by drawing a perfect circle in red paint.

Story: *"Lepus arcticus"*

Did you know that heli-skiing and heli-snowboarding are specialist types of downhill skiing and snowboarding in which the skier or snowboarder is able to access remote slopes by helicopter? This story involves the following:

- David: a professional snowboarder from Canada
- Megan: David's wife, also a professional snowboarder
- Helipro: a company that organizes heli-skiing and heli-snowboarding tours in the Kamchatka Peninsula in the northeast of Russia
- Mikhail: a cameraman who works for Helipro — he films skiers and snowboarders from helicopters

Part One

In 2015, David was snowboarding down a mountain in the Kamchatka Peninsula.[1] The snow was deep and untouched, and David started an avalanche.

▶

Unaware of the danger, he continued down the slope, moving from side to side, with the avalanche behind him getting stronger and stronger, faster and faster.

David saw the avalanche just in time.[2] But he didn't panic. He used his skill to move to the side of the avalanche and escape.

David felt lucky to be alive. He felt certain that if he hadn't escaped from the avalanche, he wouldn't have survived.

Part Two

That night, David was having drinks with his friend Mikhail.[3]

"I am lucky to be alive", said David over and over again. "If I hadn't escaped from the avalanche, I wouldn't have survived."

Mikhail said: "David. I have a surprise for you."[4] "While you were snowboarding down the mountain, I was filming from the helicopter. When you started the avalanche, I was filming. You continued down the slope, moving from side to side with the avalanche behind you getting stronger and stronger, faster and faster. You were completely unaware of the danger. Meanwhile, I was filming. You saw the avalanche just in time."

"I didn't panic", said David.

"No", said Mikhail. "You used your skill to move to the side of the avalanche and escape. And I caught it all on camera. Would you like to see the video?"

Mikhail took out his mobile phone. They watched the video over and over again. They argued about whether or not David would have survived if he hadn't escaped from the avalanche.[5]

Part Three

David returned to Canada. His wife Megan asked him how the trip was. David said: "Megan, darling, I am lucky to be alive.

I was snowboarding down a mountain. The snow was deep and untouched, and I started an avalanche. I was unaware of the danger, and I continued down the slope, moving from side to side with the avalanche behind me getting stronger and stronger, faster and faster. I saw the avalanche just in time."

"Did you panic?" asked Megan.

"No, I didn't panic", said David. "I used my skill to move to the side of the avalanche and escape. I'm lucky to be alive, I tell you. If I hadn't escaped from the avalanche, I wouldn't have survived. And Mikhail caught it all on camera. Would you like to see the video?"

David showed Megan the video and Megan noticed something that no one else had seen.[6] On the right-hand side of the screen, a confused Arctic hare runs across the slope and into the avalanche.

"The poor creature!" said Megan.

Part Four

David couldn't believe that neither he nor Mikhail had noticed the Arctic hare. He sent a message to Mikhail to tell him about it.

Now, there is nothing easier to miss than a white hare in an avalanche. Mikhail knew that and he decided to investigate. He found the exact moment in the video at which the hare disappears. He zoomed in and played it in slow motion. And he couldn't believe what he saw.[7]

Mikhail sent a message back to David. It said: "David. I think this story has a new star."

Video: "Avalanche! Run Rabbit Run!"

This story is based on a video uploaded onto Vimeo in 2015. The snowboarder, David Carrier-Porcheron, was making a video with Helipro when he accidentally set off an avalanche.

The incident was caught on camera by Mikhail Moroz, who was filming from the helicopter. But as mentioned above, the star of the video is a confused Arctic hare (*Lepus arcticus*) that runs directly into the avalanche. It kicks, it fights, and it does everything that it can to save itself from being buried by the snow. And incredibly, it manages to get to the other side, apparently unharmed. David Carrier-Porcheron is married to former pro snowboarder Megan Pischke but the story that I have written is fictionalized.

Helipro used the footage of the avalanche, snowboarder, and hare to create an advertisement. They accompanied the footage with the popular children's song "Run Rabbit Run".

The video is in two parts: Part One (00:00–00:12, using the time marker) is in real time: David Carrier-Porcheron snowboards down the slope just after setting off the avalanche. If you know where to look, you can see the Arctic hare. Part Two (00:12–00:46) repeats the video in slow motion and zooms in on the hare.

Many media outlets reported the story of the Arctic hare and you can find a lot of articles about it online.

Discussion

This story is potentially quite interactive. Here is one way that you could tell the story in the classroom. First, on the board, write the following:

- *heli-snowboarding*
- *the Kamchatka Peninsula*
- *Helipro*
- *David (a professional snowboarder)*
- *Mikhail (a cameraman who works for Helipro and films snowboarders and skiers from helicopters)*

Next, ask students the following questions:

- *Do you know what heli-skiing or heli-snowboarding is?*

- *Do you know where the Kamchatka Peninsula is?*
- *Would you prefer David's job or Mikhail's job?*

From here on, tell students the story and pause to ask the following questions or give the following tasks:

1. *What are the dangers of heli-snowboarding or heli-skiing?*

2. *Would you panic in a situation like this? Do you think that David panicked?*

3. *Can you remember what Mikhail does for a living?*

4. *What do you think Mikhail's surprise was?*

5. Show students the first part of the video (00:00–00:12) with the sound down. Ask students to choose one of the following statements and elaborate on it:
   - *I think that he would have been okay.*
   - *I think that he would have survived, but he would have been injured.*
   - *I don't think that he would have survived.*

6. *Can you guess what Megan saw?* Play the first part of the video again. It is actually very difficult to see the hare if you don't know what you are looking for. Play the video a third and fourth time. Invite students to ask you questions to work out what Megan saw.

7. *What do you think Mikhail discovered when he slowed down the video and zoomed in on the hare?*

After the story and before watching the complete video, ask students: *What do you think that Helipro decided to do with this piece of footage? What song would you choose to accompany the video?* ("I Will Survive" is a popular choice.)

► **Students as Storytellers**

As a follow-up task, ask students to imagine the story from the Arctic hare's point of view. Ask them to prepare the story that hare would tell its friends or write in its diary. Importantly, why did it run into the avalanche?

► **Tips for English Language Teachers**

Use this story to introduce or revise either of the following grammar points:

- the third conditional (*If I hadn't escaped from the avalanche, I wouldn't have survived.*)

- past continuous versus past simple (*While you were snowboarding down the mountain, I was filming from the helicopter. When you started the avalanche, I was filming.*)

▶ **Subject Connections**

- Biology and ecology: This story provides a great introduction to Arctic and Subarctic wildlife.

- Geography: This story took place on the slopes of a volcano in one of the most outstanding volcanic regions in the world. The volcanoes of Kamchatka are listed as one of Russia's twenty-six UNESCO World Heritage Sites.

- Tourism: As a sport, heli-skiing is just a few decades old. It began in Canada and involved small groups of dedicated risk-takers. Students could explore how it developed as an industry from there.

◀ 2 ▶

Withholding Information

I WONDER IF YOU know this puzzle that I remember from my childhood: A man and his son are involved in a car accident. The man dies instantly. The boy is unconscious but still alive. He is rushed to the nearest hospital in need of immediate surgery. The surgeon enters the emergency room, sees the boy, and says: "I can't operate on this boy. He is my son." Can you explain?

The stories in this book have a lot in common with puzzles like this. Many of them withhold important information - facts about the videos that they are based on. Sometimes, the stories exploit assumptions that students might make - the assumption, for example, that the surgeon in the puzzle is a man.

By withholding details about a video, we can set up an information gap between the teacher and the students. There are a number of reasons for doing this:

- It can engage students and get them curious.

- It can motivate the teacher. We all like to have a surprise up our sleeves!

- It builds in a task for the students: to speculate about the missing information.

- It further heightens what I call the moment of comparison, which I described in the introduction.

- It motivates the students to listen to the story a number of times. This can be especially important for English language learners.

- As we will see, it can be a good way of raising students' awareness of editing techniques, advertising tricks, stereotyping in the media, and more.

In this chapter, we consider different types of information about the video that we can choose to omit from the story. But first a word of advice: Unlike the surgeon puzzle, the stories in this book do not exist primarily to be solved. In fact, in many cases, a "solution" would be virtually impossible for students to find.

In Videotelling, withheld information can prompt a thinking task or provide an element of surprise. But it is just a small part of the story and should not define the activity. As is always the case, students' ideas and imagination are central to the story – not the "answer" that the video provides.

....

 All videos, materials, and resources that I refer to in this chapter can be accessed at **www.videotelling.com** For more information, see appendix 1.

....

2.1 The Richard Parker Device

If you have read Yann Martel's novel *Life of Pi* or seen the movie, the name Richard Parker will be familiar to you. Richard Parker enters the main story near the beginning of the book in spectacular fashion.

The young Pi Patel and his family have left India and are on a ship travelling to Canada. One night during the ocean voyage, they get caught in a fierce storm and the ship starts to sink. Pi finds himself alone on a lifeboat adrift from the ship. And as the ship goes down, he sees the familiar face of Richard Parker, a fellow passenger, struggling in the sea.

With all his strength, Richard Parker swims toward the lifeboat and an excited Pi encourages him to climb aboard. But Pi's initial enthusiasm quickly turns into panic and terror as he realizes what might happen with Richard on the lifeboat.

One of the remarkable things about human beings is our ability to develop images in our heads from words alone. In this scene from the book, we effortlessly imagine the sinking ship, the fierce storm, the rocking lifeboat, and the terrified Pi.

We also create an image of Richard Parker swimming toward and climbing onto the lifeboat. But why does Pi panic? What is the problem with Richard? Who is he? Is he dangerous? Intrigued, we start to speculate, explore ideas, and create our own theories.

Shortly afterwards, we are given the answer, and in an instant our own mental image is revised: Richard Parker is a fully grown, 450-pound Bengal tiger.

By simply giving the tiger a human name and withholding information, Yann Martel is able to disguise the essential element of the scene, engage the reader's curiosity, and create a more interactive reading experience. The device contributes to an unforgettable moment in the story.

When creating Videotelling stories, we can borrow from Yann Martel's technique. We can choose to give human names to non-human protagonists and disguise their true nature. In fact, we have already seen this technique used three times in chapter 1:

- "Feeding Time": It soon becomes clear that Boris and Amba are not human. So, what kind of animals are they, given that they can eat whole watermelons?

- "Eagle Eyes": The story does not mention that Elizabeth is an eagle, although it does provide clues.

- "An Act of True Love": The story makes no reference to the fact that Isabel is a car.

Fortunately, there is no shortage of online videos that star cats, dogs, bears, pigs, rabbits, and other animals. We can apply the Richard Parker device to virtually any of these.

But a word of warning: It is easy to overuse the Richard Parker device. It can work well a few times but students will quickly get wise to the trick. When I am Videotelling in my classroom, one of the first questions students ask me is: *"Are they human?"*

Story: "An Audition"

Super Chill lives in Hollywood. Today he has an audition.
He leaves his apartment and takes the elevator downstairs.
He gets on the bus and makes his way to the audition venue.

While he is on the bus, Super Chill listens to music and texts a friend to calm his nerves. He gets off the bus, waits for the lights to change, crosses the road, and walks into the audition venue. He gives his resumé and photograph to the receptionist. She asks him to take a seat. Super Chill waits in the waiting room.

After a while, they call Super Chill's name and he goes into the audition room. As requested, he takes off his clothes and he monkeys around.

> "Thank you very much. We'll call you", says a woman on the sofa. Super Chill puts back on his clothes and leaves the audition room.
>
> It's been a long day. Super Chill goes to his favourite Mexican restaurant.

Video: "Super Chill Monkey Does Hollywood"

This text describes a three-minute video that was uploaded onto a YouTube channel called "Unbuttoned Films". It features an orangutan who wears clothes, operates a mobile phone, and interacts with humans. The video is titled "Super Chill Monkey Does Hollywood".

Although most people don't realize it, the video is an advertisement. Unlike the advertisements that we are used to on TV, this one makes no explicit reference to the product. Perhaps the creators wanted to produce something that people actually want to watch, and in doing so, set up an opportunity for product placement.

And the product is there, all the way through the video. It is the Levi's jeans that Super Chill is wearing. The video contains two carefully placed close-up shots - one of the iconic Levi's red tab on the back pocket and another of the Levi's-branded metal button on the front.

With videos like this, the internet has blurred the lines between advertising and entertainment. It has given rise to what we could call stealth advertising.

Discussion

The story "An Audition" makes no reference to the fact that the protagonist is not human - an unexpected surprise for students when they come to see the video.

After telling the story, ask students to guess what Super Chill is auditioning for - a part as a model, a dancer, a stripper, an

actor? Tell students that the story describes a video on YouTube and ask them to guess what kind of video it is (a children's cartoon, a music video, an advertisement, a short film, a clip from a documentary, etc.). After that, show the video and ask students the same question: What kind of video is it? Will they realize that it is an advertisement? If so, can they identify the product?

▶ **Tips for English Language Teachers**
The story contains many present simple verbs in the third-person singular form. Write these on the board as shown below (bold words only). Tell students that you are going to use the verbs to tell them a story about a day in the life of a Hollywood performer who goes for an audition. Ask them to predict the things that he does before you tell them the story.

- *He leaves his apartment.*
- *He takes the elevator downstairs.*
- *He gets on the bus.*
- *He listens to music.*
- *He texts a friend.*
- *He gets off the bus.*
- *He waits for the lights to change.*
- *He crosses the road.*
- *He waits in the waiting room.*
- *He goes into the audition room.*
- *He takes off his clothes.*
- *He monkeys around.*
- *He puts back on his clothes.*
- *He leaves the audition room.*
- *He goes to a restaurant.*
- *He eats a burrito.*

After students have made predictions, tell them the story and then show them the video. As a follow-up, you can ask students to retell the story in the past simple tense using the verbs on the board to help them (e.g. *He left his apartment.*; *He took the elevator downstairs.*).

▶ **Subject Connections**

In science, biology, environmental studies or media studies classes, the story and video may raise other issues:

- An inaccuracy: There is a mistake in the video name – while the video title is "Super Chill Monkey Does Hollywood", the animal is an orangutan, which is an ape, not a monkey.
- An ethical issue: At a time when orangutans are endangered, some people may think that dressing them up as humans for the purpose of selling jeans is a mistake in itself. This advertisement could be used to introduce the subjects of ethics in advertising and wildlife conservation.

- Viral advertising: The video could serve as a lead-in to the subject of advertising past and present. The first official paid television advertisement was a nine-second spot commercial for Bulova watches. You can easily find it online. Students could investigate how the culture of TV advertising has changed over the years and how it has continued to change as it has moved into the internet age.

2.2 Withholding Other Facts

When creating a video-based story, there are other types of fact that we can withhold. This can engage students and give rise to a task. Here is a simple three-step idea:

1. Find a TV advertisement online. Choose something which is appropriate for your students – an advertisement that they will like. The simpler the narrative, the better.

2. Prepare a story text in which you describe the advertisement but do not make any reference to the product.

3. Describe the video to your students and ask them to guess the product.

Story: "Jamie's All-Time Favourite TV Advertisement"
I'm going to describe my favourite TV advertisement ever.
It starts with a man in the street and he's desperate.
He's running away from this big belly – this big fat hairy belly.
And the big fat hairy belly is chasing him everywhere.
And the man's running away as fast as he can.

So, to try to escape, the man jumps over a fence. But the big fat hairy belly crashes straight through the fence. It's so big, you see.

▶

▶ And then the man runs into a shopping centre (shopping mall) and he runs up the escalator. And the big fat hairy belly follows him into the shopping centre but uses a lift (elevator).

And then the man runs through a car park (parking lot). The big fat hairy belly also runs through the car park, chasing him.

Eventually, the man manages to lose the big fat hairy belly. He uses his intelligence to do so.

And all the way through the advertisement there's this crazy music - heavy metal - that goes: "Belly's gonna get you, belly's gonna get you."

It's a funny advertisement. I like it. I remember it from quite a long time ago - fifteen or twenty years ago perhaps. I can't be sure. But I'm not going to tell you what the product is. You've got to guess.

Video: "Lose the Beer Belly"

The story text is a transcription of a talking head video that I made titled "Jamie's All-Time Favourite TV Advertisement". You can see the video on my YouTube channel (see appendix 1 for instructions on how to access it). The advertisement that I describe is for Reebok running shoes. The slogan at the end of the advertisement reads "Lose the Beer Belly". You can also see the advertisement online. Search for *Belly's gonna get ya*.

Discussion

Of course, you can make use of my own video and transcript to set up this activity. But I would also suggest that you choose to use an advertisement that is meaningful to you in some way or another. Try to use an advertisement that is available on YouTube or a similar video site.

Make sure you prepare your story first - decide how you are going to tell it and what language choices you are going to use. As I did, describe the advertisement to your students without telling them what the product is. Encourage students to guess the product and then show them the advertisement.

▶ **Students as Videotellers**

Ask students to go online and find an advertisement that they like. They should then create a story in which they describe the advertisement but don't say what the product is. Later, students can share their stories and in each case, guess what the mystery products are.

Similarly, students can either describe a music video without referring to the singer, band or song, or describe a clip from a film or TV show without mentioning its title, the actors, or names of the characters. In each case, when students share their stories, the withheld facts provide interactive tasks.

2.3 Withholding Genre

In general, TV is structured and predictable. We refer to TV guides to find out what's on. We understand schedules – we usually know when to expect news reports, commercial breaks, and children's programming. We can instantly recognize quiz shows, drama, or reality TV. We probably know what to expect in a genre.

Online video is different. It is possible to click on a link to a video with very little idea about what we are going to see. Virtually anything can come out of that rectangle on your computer screen, and this has led to some interesting new genres and cultures – see, for example, "A Tale of Two Ryans" in chapter 1.

When we put a video narrative into words, genre is one of the most fundamental things that can be lost. And we can exploit this.

The following story describes a mystery video. As they listen to the story, students have to decide what the genre of the video could be.

Story: "On the Moon" ⬜

1. We start with a landscape shot of the surface of the moon. In the foreground, there are three astronauts at work. Two of them are planting a United States flag. We can hear a voice coming through the radio from mission control.

2. The camera quickly zooms in on a crater in the background of the shot. From out of the crater, climbs a huge alien monster. It lets out a terrifying roar. The astronauts flee! They run toward our point of view.

3. The monster pulls the flag out of the ground and throws it behind. It brings a giant fist down on the first astronaut and crushes the body into the ground. It picks up the second astronaut, bites off the head, and throws the body high into

the air. The monster turns to the third astronaut who is still running toward us. It grabs the astronaut with its enormous hands, crushes the body, and throws it against the ground. The music stops. As we move away from the scene, we realize that there is a fourth astronaut hiding behind a rock. The astronaut is trembling and breathing deeply, clearly terrified.

4. The monster is unaware of the presence of the fourth astronaut. It turns its back on us and is about to disappear back into its crater. But just at that moment, the astronaut lets out a little fart. Hearing this, the monster stops and turns around.

5. The music starts again and we cut to an image of a product.

6. Beside the image of the product, there is a slogan that reads: "Not for astronauts".

Video: "Beans"

As you have probably guessed, the video is an interesting advertisement. The product that it seems to be advertising is Haynes Beans. The advertisement seems to play on the fact that tinned beans are well-known for causing flatulence. However, the brand Haynes Beans does not exist. It is a fictitious brand that has cleverly been named and designed to resemble Heinz Beanz (a real product). The video is actually an advertisement for Cinesite, the visual effects company that produced it. On YouTube, the advertisement is simply titled "Beans".

Discussion

You can start this activity by eliciting as many different genres of online video as possible. Ask students to suggest types of online videos and offer some of your own. These could include the following:

- short films
- instructional videos
- advertisements
- videos made by YouTubers
- prank videos (practical jokes caught on camera)
- fail videos (videos of things going wrong)
- comedy sketches
- news reports
- presentations (TED talks, etc.)
- music videos (including unofficial fan videos)
- parody videos and remixes
- caught on camera (newsworthy events filmed with mobile phones, for example)
- TV branded content

Tell students that you are going to tell them a story that describes a mystery video from YouTube. As you tell the story, ask the students to consider what type of video you are describing. In other words, what genre does it belong to? Pause to ask for students' ideas as you read each of the six parts of the story. Here are some typical answers:

After part 1:
- footage from the Apollo missions
- a clip from a science fiction film

After part 2:
- a clip from a science fiction film
- a children's cartoon

After part 3:
- a clip from a science fiction or horror film

After part 4:
- a comedy sketch

After part 5:
- an advertisement (ask students to suggest the product)

After part 6:

- In my experience, students will usually guess that it is an advertisement for beans or some other food that causes flatulence.

After you have told the whole story, ask students whether or not it would be a good idea for a manufacturer to draw attention to the fact that their product makes you fart. Encourage students to give reasons for their answer. Opinion will probably be divided here. One of my students said she liked the honesty of this advertisement and described it as *"a breath of fresh air"*.

When you show students the video, it will be interesting to see if they realize that the product is fictitious. In my experience, the vast majority of people do not. Once students realize that there is no such product as Haynes Beans, ask them to speculate about who created the video and why. Can the genre be categorized? As was the case with "Super Chill Monkey Does Hollywood", it's an advertisement but not as we know it!

2.4 Withholding Outcomes and Endings

One of the most fundamental ways of making a story interactive is to withhold the ending and ask students to guess what happens next. I have used this device in a number of stories throughout the book. I cut the story short and ask students to predict the ending before showing them the video. The video itself will usually provide an answer. But as is the case with the following story, that isn't always the way.

Story: "Why Are You Lying on the Pavement?"

A pedestrian is walking on the pavement (sidewalk) in a street
He is not paying attention
He is not looking where he is going and suddenly . . .
He trips and falls
He gets up and sees why he fell:
Lying in the middle of the pavement is . . .
A man

The man is well-dressed and he is conscious
The pedestrian kneels down and says:
"I'm sorry. I didn't see you there. Are you okay?"

The man on the pavement replies:
"Yes. I'm fine. Please leave me alone."

The pedestrian says:
"Then why are you lying in the middle of the pavement?
I tripped over you. I could have broken my neck.
Have you been drinking? Have you fallen? Are you injured?"

The man on the pavement replies:
"No. I haven't been drinking. I haven't fallen. I'm not injured.
Please leave me alone."

"So why are you lying on the pavement?" asks the pedestrian

A crowd gathers. They ask:
"What's going on here?
Why is this man lying on the pavement?
What's wrong with him? Has he been drinking?
Has he fallen? Is he injured? Is he mad?"

The man on the pavement replies:
"I'm fine. I haven't been drinking. I haven't fallen. I'm not injured.
I'm not mad. Please leave me alone."

▶ "So why are you lying on the pavement?" asks the crowd.

A police officer arrives. He asks:
"What's going on here?
Why is this man lying on the pavement? What's wrong with him?
Has he been drinking? Has he fallen? Is he injured? Is he mad?"

The man on the pavement replies:
"I'm fine. I haven't been drinking. I haven't fallen. I'm not injured.
I'm not mad. Please leave me alone."

"So why are you lying on the pavement?" asks the police officer.

"I can't tell you. It wouldn't be right", says the man on the pavement.
"Tell us!"
"Do you really want to know?"
"Yes!"
"Okay. I'll tell you why I'm lying here. But God forgive me.
And God help us all. I am lying on the pavement because . . ."

Video: The Music Video for "Just" by Radiohead

"Why Are You Lying on the Pavement?" is based on the music video for the 1995 Radiohead single "Just". The video was directed by Jamie Thraves and was filmed near Liverpool Street Station in London. In the video, a middle-aged man walks out of his apartment and lies down on the pavement. As people gather around him, the conversation that takes place is subtitled on the screen.

At the end of the video, the man finally gives in and tells the people why he is lying there. As he delivers the crucial line, the camera zooms in on his mouth. Unfortunately for the viewer (and for your students!), the subtitles stop at that exact moment. Although his reason is left open to interpretation, we soon discover the effect that it has on the people around him:

As the camera moves away from the man, we see that everyone in the crowd has decided to join him. They too are now lying on the pavement.

Discussion

In some ways, the story "Why Are You Lying on the Pavement?" may resemble a children's story. It contains a repetitive element, which almost makes it comical. This detracts from the more serious character of the music video that it is based on. Repeated language can also be catchy and memorable.

I like to prepare for this story by drawing the outline of a figure on the classroom floor. As students enter the class, this should get them curious. You can arrange the seating so that everyone sits in a circle around the figure.

Tell students that the figure is not actually lying on the classroom floor. The figure is lying on a pavement in a street. Ask students what they would do if they found someone lying on the pavement like this. Most people will decide that their actions - to help or not to help - would depend on various circumstances. Ask your students to consider what these circumstances could be. In other words, what would it depend on? Answers could include any of the following:

- if it was during the day or at night
- if the person was a man or a woman
- if the person was young or old
- if it was in your students' own town or in an unfamiliar city
- if the person was conscious or unconscious
- if the person was scruffy or well-dressed
- if the person was from a different background or community (e.g. a fan of a rival football or hockey team)

Refer to the figure on the classroom floor and continue with the following questions: *Why do you think this person is lying on the pavement? If you were going to approach the person, what would you say?*

After the discussion, tell the story and invite students to predict how it ends. Ask students to guess what the man says at the end. After that, show the video but be prepared for mixed reactions. Some students will like the open-ended nature of the story. Others may feel disappointed.

As a follow-up activity, ask students to go online and investigate the many theories about why the man is lying on the pavement. Students might also like to see the video's unofficial sequel. In 2008, DJ and producer Mark Ronson released a cover version of the same Radiohead song. Ronson's accompanying music video uses the same subtitled format as before and develops the story of the people on the pavement further.

▶ **Tips for English Language Teachers**

The repeated lines in the story contain present perfect simple and present perfect continuous structures. You can use the story as a springboard to teach these.

▶ **Students as Filmmakers**

Before showing the music video, invite students to create short films to bring the story to life. Put students into groups and give out copies of the story. Tell them that the story should basically be the same but they are free to change the spoken words to make the dramatization more natural. They should create a script and decide how the story ends. Each group will need at least five people:

- a cameraperson
- an actor to play the pedestrian
- an actor to play the man (or woman) on the pavement
- an actor to play the crowd (In the video, this can be an individual person.)
- an actor to play the police officer

Encourage students to plan their video, choose locations (A playground would work well, for example.), and edit their work. Later, you can have a class viewing and give prizes to the best film. Appendix 4 offers technical and practical advice for teachers who are interested in setting up video tasks like this.

Story: "Terrified" ⓘ

Wendy is running down a long, blood-red corridor...
In a haunted hotel
She is wearing a dressing gown and she is holding...
A large kitchen knife

At the end of the corridor, there is...
An elevator
Wendy stops, too terrified to scream
She watches as the elevator doors open

And then...
The most terrifying sight that any human being could ever see!

📺 Video: "The PSYning"

This story describes a key scene from Stanley Kubrick's classic horror film *The Shining*. Wendy Torrance (Shelley Duvall) is trying to protect herself from her husband (Jack Nicholson), who has been possessed by evil forces and is chasing her with an axe.

In the film, the terrifying sight that Wendy sees is a slow-motion inundation of human blood, pouring out from behind the elevator doors. On YouTube, however, things are different. When the elevator doors open, we don't see blood. Instead we see South Korean musician Psy lying face down on the floor with a very odd character dancing above him. Confused? This is a comical moment from Psy's music video for his 2012 hit song "Gangnam Style".

This YouTube video was created by user IncognitusYT. It is titled "The PSYNING" and is an example of a video mashup. Video mashups bring together moments from unrelated viral videos, internet memes, film clips, TV clips, celebrity footage, interviews, and much more. By combining pre-existing video content, new meaning is created. The story "The Kuleshov Effect" in chapter 5 is based on another video mashup.

Discussion

In order to engage students from the start, tell them that you are going to describe a scene from a famous film. Ask students to try to identify the film without shouting out their answers.

Once you have told the story "Terrified", distribute little pieces of paper. After hearing the story, students should write down the following:

1. the title of the film if they think they know it (If students are too young to know the film, omit this part.)

2. their guess about the terrifying thing that Wendy sees

Ask students to hand over their little pieces of paper to you. You can then go through their ideas, find out who wrote what, and discuss the answers. Finally, let students see the video.

▶ **Students as Videotellers**

Although the song "Gangnam Style" might seem a bit dated, it will go down in history as the first-ever YouTube video to reach one billion views. Never has an artifact of popular culture spread so quickly to so many corners of the world. At the time of writing, it is still the most viewed video on YouTube. Ask students to do one of the following:

- Investigate the story behind South Korean singer Psy and his hit song "Gangnam Style".
- Describe another "Gangnam Style" parody, remix, or video mashup on YouTube. There are thousands to choose from.
- Choose another mashup video that they like. It doesn't have to be related to "Gangnam Style". Students should describe the video, refer to the constituent parts, and say how they combine to create new meaning.

▶ **Tips for English Language Teachers**
You could use the story "Terrified" to introduce, revise, or clarify adjectives which can end in -ing and -ed (terrifying versus terrified).

2.5 Withholding Incongruity

In the context of film and literature, there is nothing particularly surprising about two shipwrecked passengers alone together on a lifeboat. But when one of them is a tiger, the situation is very different. We can say that it is incongruous. I am referring to the story of the *Life of Pi*, which I mentioned at the beginning of this chapter. Other examples of incongruity might be when animals take on human roles or when humans behave like animals; things are out of context or out of place; or objects are ridiculously oversized, bizarrely irrelevant or comically weird.

Incongruity is fundamental to art and comedy. It can make us laugh or it can make us see the world in a different way. It challenges our knowledge and our expectations. As a device, it can be used to entertain, delight, shock, parody, satirize, criticize or sell.

Video is a perfect medium for creating incongruity. And Videotelling is a perfect way of hiding it. We can choose to tell the story of a video without mentioning the incongruity. This will lead to a heightened experience for students at the moment of comparison.

Story: "Lambs to the Slaughter" ⚠

Farm fresh meat
That's what the sign on the door of the truck says:
Farm fresh meat
The door slams shut and the driver starts the engine
Cattle, pigs, chickens, and lambs to the slaughter
To the slaughterhouses of the Meatpacking District
In New York City

Now, in a neighbourhood like this
Slaughterhouse trucks are a fairly common sight
But there's something strange, something sinister about this one
It's the cargo that it's carrying – the animals on board

▶ Because many of them are pushing their heads out the sides of
the truck
And they are squealing
Crying for help from the people in the street
People like you and people like me

Some stop to watch
They stand and stare, unsure about what to think
Others pretend not to notice the loud cries, the begging eyes
Perhaps they feel uneasy about what they see
One girl screams and runs away
A baby starts to cry
While teenagers take pictures with their mobile phones
Young children point and wave to the animals
But most people smile
And some even laugh
They seem to think that this is funny

So what about you?
How would you feel?
How would you react?

Video: "The Sirens of the Lambs"

"The Sirens of the Lambs" was a piece of moving art by the well-
known British street artist, Banksy. You can see a video of the
work on YouTube. Search for *The sirens of the lambs.*

Banksy uses satire and dark humour to comment on social
and political issues. On each day of October 2013, he released
a new work somewhere in New York City. "The Sirens of the
Lambs" was one of these. It consisted of a modified slaughterhouse truck with dozens of squealing, toy animals peeping
out from the gaps in the sides of the truck. As the truck drove
around the streets of New York, four puppeteers inside the
truck controlled the show.

Banksy is famous for his stencil graffiti works, which have appeared in streets and other public spaces all over the world. Many of these are controversial and have fascinating stories behind them. Most can be seen online.

Discussion

The story "Lambs to the Slaughter" makes no reference to the fact that the animals are not real. As a result, the story raises questions of meat production, animal welfare, and how humans respond - all of which can provoke discussion and possibly feelings of horror. But the story leaves out the element that might also create humour: the joke of the toy animals. In a sense, when the teacher withholds the incongruity in the story and then shows the video, students can explore the subject in layers. Here is a suggestion for using the story and video in the classroom:

1. Write the following questions on the board:
   - *What is the truck carrying? What is its cargo?*
   - *Where do you think it is going?*
   - *What is strange and unusual about the truck?*
   - *How do people react to the truck when they see it?*

2. Tell students that these questions relate to a story that you are going to tell them called "Lambs to the Slaughter". Invite students to speculate about answers to the questions before they hear the story. The story title should provide answers to the first two questions (*lambs, to the slaughterhouse*) but students will have to use their imaginations for the third and fourth questions.

3. If necessary, introduce students to any potentially problematic words or ideas in the text. For example, you could use an online map or image search site to introduce New York City's Meatpacking District.

4. Read the story and — when possible — reinforce language through the use of mime, gesture, and your voice:

- *the door slams shut* [slam your hand on the desk]
- *and they are squealing* [exaggerate a long "ee" sound]
- *young children point and wave to the animals* [demonstrate these actions with your arms and hands]

5. Read the story a second time if necessary. Refer to the questions on the board and ask students to share what they understood.

6. Add the following questions to the list on the board and ask students to think about their answers: *Some people seem to think that this is funny. Why could this be? How would you react?*

7. Tell students that the story is based on an actual event. It describes a piece of street art by an artist called Banksy. Ask: *Does anyone know about Banksy? Can anyone guess how he used a slaughterhouse truck?*

8. Show students the video. Ask them for their responses. *Does the artist have a message? How does the video make you feel?*

As a follow-up task, you could ask students to go online to find a work that they like that is attributed to Banksy. They should investigate the work and then create a story in which they describe their chosen piece, tell the story behind it, and offer a personal interpretation of it.

► **Subject Connections**

Teachers of ethics and social sciences might want to use this story and video as an opportunity to discuss food production, factory farming, animal welfare, and vegetarianism. Teachers of art could ask students to create an image of the slaughterhouse truck as they imagine it. This would be after students have heard the story but before they see the video.

Story: "Mystery Crop"

The year is 1957
It's a Monday evening in April
You are at home with your family
Somewhere in the United Kingdom[1]
You are having dinner[2]
And you are all very excited[3]
Today, you have had a special delivery:
A brand-new Decca DM4[4] television set

After eating, you do your homework, then move to the sitting room
The television is in the corner of the room
You haven't felt this excited for a long time[5]
Your father turns it on[6]
There are just two channels: BBC and ITV[7]
On BBC, there is a news programme

On that day in 1957, there is a short report from Switzerland
The report is about the harvesting of a certain crop

According to the report:
The crop usually comes from Italy
It grows on trees
After it is hand-picked, it is left to dry in the sun
It is long and thin
You have to boil it and drain it before eating[8]

After watching the news report, you feel confused[9]
You turn to your sister and say: "I didn't know it grew on trees."
"Where did you think it came from?" she asks
"I hadn't really thought about it", you reply[10]

Video: "BBC Spaghetti-Tree Hoax"

The crop in question is spaghetti. The news programme was *Panorama* - the world's longest-running current affairs programme, which is still going at the time of writing. The narrator was broadcaster Richard Dimbleby. The date was April 1st. It is believed that this was the first time that television was used for an April Fool's Day hoax.

The report reached an estimated eight million people, many of whom were probably left confused by the images of a Swiss family sitting down to enjoy a meal of hand-picked spaghetti. According to the story, many viewers phoned the BBC the following day to question the authenticity of the news story. Others asked for more information about spaghetti cultivation and how they could grow their own spaghetti trees. Some viewers failed to see the funny side and criticized the BBC for broadcasting the report on what was supposed to be a serious factual programme.

Discussion

You can make this story interactive by pausing to ask questions as you tell it. For example:

1. *Where are you in the United Kingdom?* (Give students the choice to decide and state where they imagine themselves to be.)

2. *What are you eating for dinner?* (Remember - it is 1957 and you are in the United Kingdom. No pizza, sushi, or ready-made meals!)

3. *Can you guess why you are excited?*

4. *Can you guess what a Decca DM4 is?* (If students have mobile devices with online access, you could ask them to investigate this online.)

5. *Who has the remote control?* (A trick question - there isn't one!)

6. *How many channels were there on British TV back then?*

7. *What sort of programme would you expect to see in 1957?*

8. *Can you guess what the crop is?*

9. *You are confused by the report. Can you guess why?*

10. *Can you guess the exact date that this report was broadcast?*

Focus on the mystery crop. Ask students to give their ideas about what it could be. When I have used the story in class, typical guesses included asparagus, rice, wheat, carrots, and sun-dried tomatoes.

After students have given their ideas, ask them if they would like to see the *Panorama* report. Show the video and tell the story behind it. You can then ask students to imagine how they might have reacted. Also, ask whether they think it is right for a respected organization like the BBC to play tricks on its viewers.

▶ Students as Videotellers

It is easy to find references online to other TV-related April Fool's hoaxes. For example, in 1962, Swedish TV showed viewers how to get colour images from a black-and-white TV set by holding a nylon stocking in front of the screen. And in 2008, the BBC reported on a newly discovered colony of flying penguins. Ask students to investigate and report on a story that they like.

▶ Tips for English Language Teachers

When guessing what the mystery crop is, you could use this as an opportunity to use language of speculation:

- *It could be asparagus.*
- *It might be carrots or tomatoes.*
- *It must be something that needs a lot of sunlight.*

- *It can't be tomatoes. Tomatoes aren't long and thin.*
- *It definitely can't be spaghetti.*

You can also use this story to explore the grammar of countable and uncountable nouns. The five crop facts in the story refer to *it* rather than *they* or *them* (*It grows on trees.*; *You have to boil and drain it before eating.*). This fact would suggest that we are dealing with an uncountable noun (like *asparagus, rice,* or *wheat*) as opposed to a countable noun (like *carrots, potatoes,* or *sun-dried tomatoes*).

► **Subject Connections**

The story could be used by teachers of modern history. You could use it to introduce the topic of life in post-war Europe with a focus on food. Perhaps students could interview their grandparents or elderly neighbours to find out what life was like during that time. For many families, the fifties was a decade of domestic change. In Britain, food rationing ended in 1954 – just three years before the spaghetti-tree hoax. By the end of the decade, food was more varied, and fridges, food processors, electric cookers (stoves), and other household appliances were commonplace.

The story may also interest teachers of media studies. It could be used to introduce the topic of television through the ages. The BBC has a resource called the BBC Genome Project, which you can find online — see appendix 1 for access information. The website provides BBC television scheduling information from October 1936. Perhaps students could find the day they were born and create a summary of what was on TV in Britain that day.

Story: "Unusual Recipe"

The following story describes a recipe for a mysterious dish. However, I have rearranged the letters of the ingredients to create anagrams. These are in bold and will be explained later.

So, first of all, turn on the gas, place a pot of water on the heat, and add some **salty pieces** to the water. Once the water has started to boil, add a handful of **sick pup ticks**. After boiling for about six minutes, the **sick pup ticks** should look like rubber bands. This means that it is ready. Drain the **sick pup ticks** in a colander.

To prepare the sauce, heat some **filo** in a frying pan. Chop up a clove of **buck bruise** and add it to the hot **filo**. Then add three large, ripe **chip unisons** and squash them with a wooden spoon. Leave the sauce to simmer but don't forget to stir it regularly.

Next, take a **bridal loll**, chop it up finely, and add it to the sauce. Add some **cedi** to sweeten the sauce and then melt in some **pintoes tots**.

Finally, transfer the **sick pup ticks** to a plate and add a good-sized spoonful of sauce. Grate some **owlo** on top, season with **gritlet**, light a candle, sit down, and enjoy your meal.

Video: "Western Spaghetti"

The story is based on a short film called "Western Spaghetti" by PES, a stop-motion animator. PES is famous for animating everyday objects in unusual situations. The video provides a detailed demonstration of how to make a dish called Western Spaghetti. However, this is not a meal that you would want to eat. All of the ingredients are inedible. They are as follows:

salty pieces	plastic eyes
sick pup ticks	pick-up sticks
filo	foil
buck bruise	Rubik's Cube
chip unisons	pincushions
bridal loll	dollar bill
cedi	dice
pintoes tots	Post-it notes
owlo	wool
gritlet	glitter

Discussion

Before you use this story in class, you might need to find out how much students know about cooking. Ask them if they ever cook and if so, what. Do they ever watch cookery (cooking) shows? Then ask students if they can tell you all of the ingredients that you would use to make spaghetti and tomato sauce (from scratch - not from a jar!). Elicit these and write them on the board. Basic ingredients will include the following: spaghetti, oil, tomatoes, onion, garlic, herbs, and salt and pepper. Once you have done that, proceed as follows:

1. Write the anagrams (*salty pieces, sick pup ticks,* etc.) on the board but don't tell students that they are anagrams.

2. Tell students that you are going to read them a short story that describes how to prepare a mystery recipe. Tell them that all of the ingredients have been replaced with nonsense words and phrases, the ones that you have written on the board. As you read out the story, students should

think about what the actual ingredients are and write down their ideas.

3. Read the story two or three times and then let students compare their ideas in a discussion. Standard answers may include salt, pasta or spaghetti, oil, garlic, tomatoes, basil or oregano, sugar, butter or cream, cheese, pepper.

4. After taking feedback, tell students how many ingredients they guessed correctly. This will almost certainly be zero.

5. Tell students that the recipe is based on a short film by an animator called PES, who likes to use everyday objects in unusual places. Tell them that none of the ingredients is edible. Tell them that the ingredients on the board are actually anagrams. Give them a couple of minutes to look at the anagrams and start to think about what the mystery ingredients could be. You can provide clues if you like. For example, tell them that a "bridal loll" is flat and green, and doesn't grow on trees.

6. Show students the video and then ask them to solve the anagrams. In order to do this, they will have to recall all the objects that they saw.

As a follow-up task, students could invent their own silly recipes made with everyday inedible objects. To date, I have had students write recipes for soap soup, stationery pie, and grilled shoes with microchips.

▶ **Tips for English Language Teachers**
This activity can be quite difficult for learners of English. In this case, rather than telling the story yourself, you could adapt the text and turn it into a missing-ingredient gap fill. Give out copies of the adapted story text and ask students to fill in the gaps. Let them

compare their answers and then work on them together. Finally show students the video and let them see how many ingredients they guessed correctly.

If students go on to write a story of their own, give them copies of the "Unusual Recipe" story. The text contains a lot of useful language that English learners will be able to incorporate into their own recipe stories – phrases such as *first of all,* and imperative verbs, such as *add, drain,* and *heat.*

In "Mystery Crop", students get spaghetti when they don't expect it. In "Unusual Recipe", students expect spaghetti but don't get it. Videotelling allows us to withhold incongruity and this can create a greater impact when students eventually see the video.

The following two stories relate to two more videos that have something in common: They both make use of the same incongruity device. Although the incongruities will be immediately apparent when you see the videos, the stories have been written in such a way as to hide the device. In order to hide the incongruity, careful language choices had to be made. We will speak more about that in the discussion. As you read the stories, ask yourself what the incongruity could be.

Stories: "Catch of the Day" and "Predator and Prey" ⓘ

Part One: Catch of the Day

The captain stands at the ship's wheel, cigar in mouth. Down below, crew members scrub the decks and prepare the nets.

The radar system picks up a shoal directly in front of the ship. The captain sounds the alarm and the crew members take their stations.

As the ship circles the shoal, harpoons are fired.
Victims are netted, pulled on board, beaten, cut, and skinned.

The ship docks at a city harbour and the catch is sold to a trader.
At the factory, the meat is processed and homogenized. Nothing
is removed but many things are added: preservatives, stabilizers,
flavour enhancers, bulking agent...

Small individual batches of the mixture are squeezed onto
a conveyor belt. They are compressed into biscuits, each one
shaped as a miniature version of what it used to be. Unlike in the
victims' final moments in life, however, these replicas wear little
smiles on their faces.

After packaging, the boxes are shipped and distributed. They are
delivered to supermarkets and pet shops all over the country.

Part Two: Predator and Prey
This spectacular piece of footage was shot on the grassy plains
of Botswana in southern Africa. It shows the struggle between
a predator and its prey – a classic case of hunter and hunted.

Since the beasts prefer the weeds of the flat plain, they spend
long periods in the open. And here, they risk attack from hunters.
But there is safety in numbers.

The camera pans across the herd. The beasts stand upright
and alert under the African sun. Apart from the constant chewing
and the occasional twitch, they are motionless.

And then, the dark shape of the predator appears, creeping
slowly through the long grass. The herd shows signs of panic
and restlessness. Aware that he has been spotted, the predator
charges forward and the herd disperses quickly.

▶

> After a few unsuccessful attempts, the predator manages to single out an individual – an older, slower member of the group perhaps. The chase lasts for only a few seconds.
> Tired and exhausted, the victim falls.
>
> After feasting greedily on the carcass, the predator sleeps. It will be two days before he hunts again.

Videos: "King Rat" by Modest Mouse and "Jockeys in the Wild" from *Big Train*

The stories "Catch of the Day" and "Predator and Prey" relate to videos from very different genres. But despite the differences, they both make use of the same device: animals and humans swap roles.

The story "Catch of the Day" is based on the music video for "King Rat" by us rock band Modest Mouse. The video was conceived by actor Heath Ledger, a friend of the band. The video was released in 2009, the year after Ledger's untimely death.

The animated video shows a crew of whales, dolphins, and oversized fish aboard a ship. They move in on a shoal of humans, harpoon them, and skin them alive. Despite the fact that the video is created with animation, the images can be quite shocking. If you want to play it in class, it is essential to take extra time to consider how to approach it. For example, I would warn students that they might find the images quite disturbing. Find out if there is anyone in the class who would prefer not to see it, and invite those students to leave the room or at least close their eyes during the following two moments that are particularly graphic: when the first human is harpooned (3:00–3:10) and when one of the humans is skinned alive (3:40–4:10).

The story "Predator and Prey" relates to a sketch from the BBC comedy show *Big Train*, which was broadcast in 1998. The style of comedy comes straight from the books of the influential Monty Python group – bizarrely irreverent and very silly! The predator was the American musician named Prince and the prey is a herd of jockeys. Of course, not everyone will appreciate the humour here. As well as being quite British, there may be a generational aspect to consider. The style of humour may be less meaningful to today's teenagers.

Discussion

You can tell these stories to your students or hand out photocopies of the texts. Tell students that the stories relate to videos that can be seen on YouTube and that the videos have something in common. Ask students to listen to or read the stories carefully and think about the videos. What could the videos have in common?

In my experience, students will often guess that the stories relate to video clips from documentaries that involve hunting. In this case, tell students that the videos belong to very different genres and neither is a documentary.

This is actually a very difficult task. Encourage students to ask you questions and not to give in too easily. Even if they don't get the answer, it is still a valuable thinking task in itself. You could give them a clue by clarifying that, although the texts would appear to describe animals, there is no specific reference to what kind of animal they are. In creating the stories, I avoided mentioning the animals by using words like *victim*, *shoal*, *herd*, *beast*, *predator*, and *prey*. When creating a story text, taking time to make good language choices is an important part of the process.

Finally, show students the videos and they will see the withheld incongruity device: humans take the place of animals. This is a simple idea that creates a remarkably different effect in each video. Heath Ledger was opposed to illegal whale hunts that take place off the coast of Australia. By depicting the victims as human, Ledger is clearly trying to arouse feelings of horror and empathy within us and raise awareness of the whaling practices. As for the second video, it is less obvious what it sets out to achieve. I would speculate that the team behind the video want to make us laugh by setting up a situation which is as wildly absurd and silly as possible. For me, the serious tone of the narrator's voice also contributes to the comedy. Perhaps your students can offer interpretations of their own.

▶ **Tips for English Language Teachers**

"Catch of the Day" and "Predator and Prey" contain many phrases that may be unfamiliar to students. Before telling the stories or giving out the texts, write some of these phrases on the board:

- *creeping slowly through the long grass*
- *they risk attack*
- *safety in numbers*
- *crew members*
- *the radar system*
- *the herd shows signs of panic*
- *to single out an individual*
- *prepare the nets*
- *to feast greedily on a carcass*
- *scrub the decks*
- *harpoons are fired*
- *the grassy plains of Botswana*
- *a shoal*
- *to dock at a harbour*

Tell students that you are going to give them two stories: one called "Catch of the Day" and the other called "Predator and Prey". Ask students to predict what the stories are about and then guess what phrase belongs to which story. Let students have access to dictionaries for this, if possible.

▶ Students as Videotellers

There are many stories in this book that withhold incongruity in videos that they describe (e.g. "Halloween Horror Story" in chapter 1, "Lambs to the Slaughter" and "Unusual Recipe" in this chapter, and "Left on the Shelf" in chapter 4). As a follow-up, draw students' attention to the devices that these videos exploit and ask them to do the following:

- *Find a piece of visual material which makes use of an incongruity device (e.g. a short film, a piece of art, an advertisement, a photograph).*
- *Describe the visual material and describe the incongruity device.*
- *Suggest why the incongruity device is there (e.g. for purposes of comedy, parody, satire, criticism).*
- *Try to describe the thoughts, feelings, and emotions that the device creates in the minds of the audience members.*

▶ Subject Connections

The ideas that are set out in these stories might interest teachers of art, media, and film studies. They may also be relevant to teachers of psychology. Popular theories of why we find jokes funny often involve the concept of incongruity. Other theories involve superiority (for example, think of people slipping on banana skins) and Freudian ideas (dark humour and double entendres).

◀ 3 ▶

Questioning

ERHAPS THE STANDARD image of storytelling is of a
monologue: a single speaker and a group of silent lis-
teners. As we have already seen, that doesn't have to
be the case. In the classroom, a story can provide a framework
for dialogue – an opportunity for everyone to share ideas. By
asking questions, it is possible to turn a story into a whole-class
discussion with learning opportunities along the way.

Of course, this is easier said than done. Success can depend
on a lot of factors, some of which can be beyond the teacher's
control. These include having a good classroom rapport as well
as engaged, semi-orderly, and responsive students (note that
appendix 2 offers suggestions for dealing with impatient, dis-
orderly, and silent students).

But success can also depend on good preparation. When
planning a story, we can consider the following:

- What questions are we going to ask students?
- When are we going to ask them?
- What techniques can we use to manage a discussion effectively?

Finally, and perhaps most importantly, success will depend on our ability to respond effectively to the answers that students offer. It is here that storytelling becomes an improvisatory art, and I feel that this is one of the most important skills for any teacher to develop.

When asking questions, we can address the group as a whole or individuals within it. However, there are other possibilities for managing and maximizing student interaction. Throughout this chapter, you will find a number of ideas for interaction techniques that you can use in combination with the questions that you ask.

 All videos, materials, and resources mentioned in this chapter can be accessed at **www.videotelling.com** For more information, see appendix 1.

3.1 Types of Questions

As mentioned before, although students hear the same story, they will all experience it in different ways. By asking questions, we can invite individuals to explore and share aspects of their internal narratives.

Asking questions can also serve other purposes. Quite simply, questions can keep an audience engaged and prevent students from falling asleep! We can use questions to reduce teacher input and break up a story to make it easier to comprehend. Perhaps most importantly, questions can invite students to participate and interact in a number of ways:

- by sharing their knowledge
- by sharing their experiences and stories
- by personalizing the stories
- by discussing issues and sharing opinions
- by making predictions
- by demonstrating their understanding of language, concepts, and plot
- by analyzing, evaluating, inferring, and reflecting (higher-order thinking)

As you read the following three stories, consider the teacher-to-student questions that you could ask if you were telling the stories in your classroom. In each case, consider key points of your approach:

- What question would you ask?
- At what point would you ask it?
- What purpose or function could it serve? (You can refer to the list above.)

After each story, I will offer some ideas.

Story: "An Embarrassing Phone Call" (!)

[1] Mr. Barrows is a teacher with a pet hate: mobile phones that ring in class.

Mr. Barrows has a class policy for his students: if any mobile phone goes off in class, you have to answer it on loudspeaker so that everyone can hear your call.[2]

Mr. Barrows has a student called Taylor. She sits near the front of the class. Today she is expecting a call.[3]

Her phone rings.[4]

"Answer it on loudspeaker!" says Mr Barrows.

Taylor answers the call on loudspeaker so that everyone can hear.

"Hello?"

▶

"Hello. Taylor? I am calling from the pregnancy testing centre. I just wanted to let you know that the results of your test are positive."[5]

Mr. Barrows tries to interrupt: "Taylor, please take that call outside."

Taylor doesn't seem to hear him and the call continues. Things get even worse as the caller continues.[6]

"We understand that you don't know who the father is. But please don't worry. We provide counselling in situations like this."

"Thank you very much. I'll call back later", says Taylor as she hangs up the phone.[7]

An embarrassed Mr. Barrows looks at Taylor and says: "I want to apologize. I shouldn't have made you answer that call on loudspeaker. I'm very sorry."

Taylor replies: "That's okay. I've been expecting that call and I was prepared for it. I even know what I'm going to call the baby if it's a girl – April."

Video: "Best Classroom April Fool's Prank Ever"

The story is based on the video "Best Classroom April Fool's Prank Ever". In many English-speaking countries, April 1st is traditionally the day when people play practical jokes on each other. In 2014, Stephen Barrows's students played a practical joke on him.

The video was filmed secretly from the back of the class by students Josh Weiland and Molly Denny. It starts with an explanation of the teacher's policy that phones that ring in class must be answered on speakerphone.

After Taylor Nefcy's excellent performance, the video ends with Mr. Barrows thanking his class for a great joke by telling them: "I'll treasure that!" To date, the video has been viewed over fifty million times.

Discussion

Before telling the story, you could start by giving your students the following isolated story items. In other words, the following are key words and phrases that are pulled out from the story:

- *"Answer it on loudspeaker!"*
- *an embarrassing phone call*
- *an embarrassed teacher*
- *an embarrassed student*
- *April* (the girl's name)

Ask the students to guess what happens in the story but don't tell them that it is based on a video. From there on, you could tell the story and pause to ask any of the following questions:

1. *What is the code of conduct regarding mobile phone use in our class?* If mobile phones are a problem in your school, ask students to think of possible solutions. Students often have a tendency to forget classroom rules. This provides a good opportunity to remind them.

2. *Do you think that Mr. Barrows's mobile phone policy is a good idea? Why? Why not?* At this stage, you could conduct a "hands-up poll" (This activity is explained in appendix 3.). This simple technique allows students to respond to certain questions that we ask. Ask students to raise their hands if they think that Mr Barrow's policy is a good idea. Then ask them to raise their hands if they think not. Then ask for reasons.

3. *Who do you think Taylor is expecting a call from?* If you used the isolated story items idea, students will already know that the phone call is embarrassing in nature. This will make the question less open-ended.

4. *What does Mr. Barrows say when Taylor's phone rings?* When you ask this question, students have to make a connection

with a phrase that they have already encountered – "Answer it on loudspeaker!" – and bring the phrase into play.

5. *How do you think Taylor reacts? How do you think Mr. Barrows reacts?*

6. *The call gets even worse. Can you guess what happens next?*

7. *What do you think happens when Taylor hangs up the phone? How would you react if you were the student? How would you react if you were the teacher?*

Finally, tell students that the story is based on a YouTube video that went viral in 2014. Ask students to guess on which date it was filmed or, if necessary, tell them about the tradition of playing practical jokes on people on April 1st. Finally, show students the video.

▶ Students as Storytellers

As a follow-up task, ask students to tell the story of a time when they played a practical joke on someone or when they were the victim of a practical joke. If they were the victim, how did they react? Did they take the joke as well as Mr. Barrows did?

▶ Subject Connections

For history or social studies, you could use this story to set up a project or activity in which students investigate the origins of April Fool's Day and where in the world it is celebrated.

▶ Tips for English Language Teachers

You can use this story to teach the following phone-related vocabulary:

- *to go off/to ring*
- *to answer a call (on loudspeaker or speakerphone)*
- *to be expecting a call*
- *to take a call outside*
- *the caller*
- *I'll call you back.*
- *to hang up*

Story: "The Story of David and Matthew"

David is an English gentleman. And like many English gentlemen, he is a creature of habit.[1] Every day, David leaves his house and goes to buy a scratch card.[2,3]

[4] Now, despite the fact that David buys a scratch card almost every day, he has never won anything – absolutely nothing.

Today, as always, David leaves his home and goes to the shop.[5] When he opens the shop door, a bell rings to let the shopkeeper know that a customer has entered. And the shopkeeper's name is Matthew.

David and Matthew greet each other.

"Matthew?"

"David."[6]

David walks across the shop floor. He puts his hand in his pocket, takes out a coin, and places it on the counter. Matthew takes the coin and gives a scratch card to David. David takes another coin out of his pocket and starts to scratch.

And today, for the first time ever, "Ka-ching!"[7] David wins £50,000.[8,9]

David picks up the scratch card, tears it in half, and walks out of the shop.[10]

Video: "Blind Luck"

The story is based on a short film titled "Blind Luck" by James Sieradzki. The film was shortlisted for a Virgin Media Shorts award. The story that you tell your students withholds some key information from the short film. When students watch the video, they will discover the key plot points:

- David is blind so cannot see that he has a winning scratch card.

- Matthew does not tell David that he has a winning scratch card. Matthew wants to keep it for himself and tries to trick David by saying: "Better luck next time."

- Thinking that the scratch card has no value, David says: "Oh well!" and quickly tears it in half. This means that no one can claim the winnings of £50,000.

In order for students to appreciate this story, you might need to explain the following:

- In the United Kingdom, a newsagent's shop sells newspapers, magazines, cigarettes, lottery tickets, scratch cards, confectionery (candies), and snacks. In class, you could use an image search to show pictures of a typical British newsagent's shop to students.

- Scratch cards are sometimes called *scratchies*, *scratch-and-win*, or *instant lottery cards*. You scratch off areas on the card with a coin to find out whether or not you have won a prize.

- If you want to buy a scratch card or lottery ticket in the United Kingdom, you have to be sixteen or older.

- The prize, £50,000 or fifty thousand pounds sterling, is a considerable sum of money. At the time of writing, it would be enough to buy three or four new family cars - depending on how expensive your tastes are. When you tell this story, you could convert this amount into a currency that your students are more familiar with.

Discussion

Here are some example questions that you could ask as you tell students "The Story of David and Matthew":

1. *There is something that David buys at the same time every day. Can you guess what it is?* React to students' guesses and give them clues accordingly. For example: *The thing that David buys isn't a newspaper or a magazine. But it is made of paper.* If students suggest that it is a ticket, ask them to suggest as many types of ticket as possible (e.g. bus, train, cinema, lottery).

2. *Do you or your parents buy lottery tickets or scratch cards? How often? Have you or they ever won anything?* This is an ideal moment to invite students to share any stories they have about lottery tickets or scratch cards. Although they may be too young to buy these, you can find out if they intend to do so when they are old enough.

3. *Do you think that it is good or bad to buy lottery tickets or scratch cards? Why or why not?* At this point, you could use the "Left Side, Right Side" idea, which is described in appendix 3. Ask students to move to one side of the room or another, according to whether they think that lottery tickets or scratch cards are a good idea. From there, ask students from different sides of the room to pair up and discuss their differences of opinion.

4. *Right, let's get back to David. Let's see if you can guess how this sentence finishes: Despite the fact that David buys a scratch card almost every day...* This question may be of particular interest to English language teachers. It allows you to focus on the meaning of the phrase *despite the fact that*, and then elicit language and ideas from students.

5. *Where would you buy a scratch card (in your country)? Where would you buy a scratch card in the UK?* This allows you to check and clarify a cultural point noted earlier.

6. *How do you think they greet each other? Are they happy to see each other?* On the board, write: *Matthew?/David.* Ask for volunteers to act out this exchange. Ask one student to be David and one student to be Matthew. Ask them to explore the different emotions that can be conveyed from these two words. How would it sound if they were really happy to see each other? How would it sound if they were not?

7. *Today, for the first time ever, "Ka-ching!" What does that mean?* After students conclude that David wins something, you can ask: *Can you guess how much David wins?* For English language learners, this is a good way to practise big numbers. For each guess, give students feedback by saying *higher* or *lower*. Do this until they arrive at the actual figure of £50,000.

8. *How much is that worth in your currency?* You could use an online currency converter to calculate this.

9. *What would you do if you won that money?* Although this is a good personalization question for many students, it will be less meaningful to younger learners who don't yet have a grasp of the value of money. In such cases, you could simply ask what they would buy if they won some money. For English language learners, the question provides an opportunity to practise second conditional structures (e.g. *If I won the lottery, I would buy a yacht.*).

10. *Would you like to know what David does? David picks up the scratch card, tears it in half, and walks out the shop. Can you guess why?*

After exploring ideas, show students the short film "Blind Luck".

► Subject Connections

In my experience, most people will consider Matthew's actions to be completely inexcusable. For teachers of ethics, it can be interesting to explore this in some detail. Ask students to discuss the following questions:

- *If you were in Matthew's position, would you be a tiny bit tempted to do what he did? If so, what would stop you from doing so?*
- *Can you think of any circumstances that would justify Matthew's actions?* (For example, perhaps Matthew's mother desperately needed a £50,000 operation and Matthew wanted to find the money to pay for it.)
- *Do you think that Matthew changed in any way as a result of this experience? If so, how and why? And if not, why not?*

Story: "Can't Hug Every Cat" ⓘ

[1] This is the story of two women with two very different obsessions.

Part One: Debbie

Debbie is in her early twenties. She is sociable, intelligent, and attractive. She is single and she is looking for love.[2]

One day, Debbie decides to try online dating.[3] She registers with a popular dating site. She fills in forms and ticks boxes. The site gives Debbie the option to upload a short video about herself.[4] She decides to do it.

Debbie considers what she should say in the video[5] – her likes, her dislikes, the sort of man she is looking for. But what about her obsession? Should she mention that?

Debbie turns on her video camera and presses record. She smiles for the camera and starts to speak.

▶

"Hello, my name is Debbie. I have never tried online dating before so I'm nervous and excited at the same time. So what can I tell you about myself? Well, I am a business studies graduate. I am in my early twenties. What else? Well, I ... love ... cats ..."

Oh dear! Those three little words are enough to bring out Debbie's obsession. The dam bursts and her head is flooded with cat images and cat memories:
Cat whiskers, cat noses, cat ears
Fat cats, stray cats, homeless cats
Cats in boxes, cats in bow ties, cats on rainbows, cats on YouTube[6]
Standing Cat, DJ Cat, Keyboard Cat, Dramatic Cat

As Debbie's mind fills with cats, her eyes fill with tears. She pauses to dry them. She takes a deep breath and explains:

"Sorry. I just get so emotional when I think about cats. I love cats. I love every kind of cat. I want to hug all of them but I can't. I can't hug every cat. That would be crazy. But I want to. I want to. I want to."

The tears come back. Debbie stops. She turns off the camera and goes to bed. She'll delete the video in the morning.[7]

Part Two: Cara

Debbie and Cara seem to have a lot in common: they are the same age, they both studied business, they live in the same city, and they even look similar.

But in most ways, they are completely different. And their paths have only ever crossed once before. That was on June 4, 2011[8] – the day that Cara uploaded Debbie's "I Love Cats" video onto her new YouTube channel.[9]

So why did she do that?

Well, although Cara isn't obsessed with cats, she does have an addiction that many of us will be familiar with:[10] social media.[11]

Every day, Cara spends hours on Snapchat, Instagram, Facebook, Pinterest, YouTube, and Twitter. When she uploaded Debbie's video, she knew that it would get some views, likes, and comments from her friends.

But Cara had no idea just how popular the video would be. By the end of 2011, it had been viewed almost twenty million times on YouTube. It was the viral video of the year.

Debbie became a mysterious online celebrity. Many laughed at her. Many felt sorry for her. Some even claimed to have similar cat obsessions.

As for Cara, thousands of people subscribed to her YouTube channel. But she also received a lot of online hate and even a few death threats. For Cara, this was a lesson on the power of the internet and perhaps more importantly, the power of cats.[12]

Video: "eHarmony Video Bio"

On YouTube, Debbie's video is titled "eHarmony Video Bio" and can be seen at Cara Hartmann's YouTube channel (which is called "hartmanncara"). In case you didn't realize, Debbie and Cara are the same person.

According to an online interview, which you can access on the accompanying website (see appendix 1 for information), Cara Hartmann created the video late one night. She filmed it in one take, uploaded it onto YouTube, and intended it only for her friends and family. She never expected it to go viral.

In the interview, she said: "I couldn't believe people thought it was real and how angry it made them when they figured out it was a fake. I've probably blocked over two hundred people on Twitter, Facebook, and YouTube because of death threats and disgusting sexual comments. It's pretty funny but also really disturbing."

Discussion

This story opens up many possible issues for discussion. These include online dating, online safety, privacy, honesty, social media addiction, and — of course — cats.

Start by telling students that you are going to tell them a story about two people with two different obsessions. From there on, tell the story and pause to ask any of the following questions:

1. *Can you give an example of an obsession? What is the difference between an obsession and a passion?*

2. *Debbie is looking for love. What do you think she should do about it? What options does she have?*

3. *Do you think that online dating is a good idea or a bad idea? What do you think are the advantages and disadvantages of online dating?* At this stage, you could set up a "pyramid discussion" - an idea that is described in appendix 3. Put students into pairs and ask them to consider precautions to take if meeting people online. Pairs then form groups of four to compare their ideas. Groups of four then form groups of eight, and so on. Eventually, you will have the whole class together again in a single group discussion.

4. *Do you think she should choose the option to make a video? Why? Why not?*

5. *What sort of information should she include in the video? Do you think that she should mention her obsession? Why? Why not?*

6. *How many cats on YouTube can you name?* If your students know YouTube well, have a competition. Put them into groups, give them two minutes, and ask them to write down as many YouTube cats as possible. Apart from the

suggestions in the story, there are many others to choose from: Nyan Cat, Ninja Cat, Pianist Cat, OMG Cat, the Talking Cats, Simon's Cat, Zero Gravity Cat, Barking Cat, Toilet Trained Cat, Angry Cat, Hunchback Cat, Patty Cake Cats, Bowling Cats, and — of course — cats and cucumbers.

7. *Can you guess what happens next?*

8. *Can you guess what happened on that day?*

9. *Would you like to see the video?* After showing the video, ask students: *What do think of this video? Should we feel sorry for Debbie? Is it right to laugh at her? Why or why not?*

10. *What do you think Cara's addiction could be?*

11. *Is there anyone here who thinks that they might also be addicted to social media? How many social media sites are you on? How much time a day do you think you spend on these sites? Would you say that this is time wasted? Why or why not?*

12. *What do you think about Cara's actions? Can you guess how she did it? Do you think that Cara was clever in producing such a successful video? Why or why not? Why do you think this video was so popular?*

▶ **Tips for English Language Teachers**

Before using this story, there is some internet-related vocabulary that students will need to know:

- *online dating*
- *online hate*
- *an online celebrity*
- *a viral video*
- *social media*
- *views, likes, and comments*

- *to register with a dating site*
- *to subscribe to a YouTube channel*
- *to upload a video*
- *to delete a video*

▶ Students as Videotellers

The story of Cara Hartmann's video is not complete without a mention of the song and music video "Can't Hug Every Cat". It was created by the Gregory Brothers – a New York–based group that is famous on YouTube for "songifying" (their term) famous viral videos:

- "The Bed Intruder Song!!!"
- "Double Rainbow Song!!"
- "Backing Up Song"
- "Best NASCAR Prayer Ever"
- "Happy Chewbacca Mask"

All of these videos have strong stories behind them, and students could choose one to investigate. The Gregory Brothers' YouTube channel is called "schmoyoho".

▶ Subject Connections

This story can introduce the topics of internet dating, online safety, and online privacy. As more and more young people use internet dating sites and apps, this story is an opportunity to address the dangers of meeting strangers online and discuss the best safety precautions to take. Also, although Debbie's character is fictitious, there are many cases in which personal videos have ended up online for the world to see. In some cases, this can destroy lives.

Teachers of media studies could use the story as a way to set up a project where students research the history of cats on the internet. Although this may seem like a trivial topic, online cats are big business. Incidentally, the first ever cat video is thought to have been made in 1894 at Thomas Edison's studio – Black Maria Studio in New Jersey, USA. It features two cats boxing. You can easily find it online.

3.2 The Storyteller's Challenge

Perhaps the most difficult part of asking questions is responding naturally to the wide range of students' answers. This requires improvisatory skills. It involves showing interest in ideas and looking for ways to develop them further.

One reason why this is so difficult is that the storyteller/teacher is always at a disadvantage. We already know the story and we have already seen the video. And this knowledge can easily influence us. It can cause us to evaluate students' ideas not for what they are but according to whether or not they fit with the "facts".

In order to interact naturally with students, the challenge for us is to try to forget the "answers" that the story or video provide and to be more open to the exploration and development of students' ideas. In this section, we will look at two stories and further develop these points about student interaction.

Story: "A Man, a Woman, a Vase"
For this story, we are going to do things a little bit differently. Rather than having the story as text, the story is provided by a series of illustrations based on stills (non-moving images) from a short film. As you look at the images, become aware of the questions that form in your mind and the answers that you imagine.

Video: "Conversation Piece"

The stills are taken from a short film called "Conversation Piece", which was written and directed by Joe Tunmer.

At the beginning of the film, the man puts on a jazz record by Rex Stewart, which is also called *Conversation Piece*. It is a slow instrumental piece of music, which consists of an improvised call and response between a cornet (an instrument similar to a trumpet) and a lower-pitched, muted trumpet.

The conversation in question starts when the woman sees the broken vase. It then leads to accusation, retaliation, and reconciliation. And although we see the emotional interaction between the couple – the anger, the tears, and the tenderness – the audio track provides no spoken words. Rather, the actors' mouth movements perfectly match the accompanying notes and phrases that are provided by the cornet (her) and the trumpet (him).

Importantly, the fact that we don't know what the man and woman are saying means that many of the questions asked will have no answer. Asking open-ended questions like these is a great way to put us in the right frame of mind for dialogic storytelling. It allows us to respond to students' answers and ideas without being influenced by the "facts" of the video.

Discussion

For this activity, you can play the video with the sound down, pause it at key moments, and then ask students questions. Or you can create a slideshow of stills using an image capture application. Suggestions for these applications are provided on the accompanying website (see appendix 1 for information).

I would suggest that you focus on the relationship and conversation between the man and the woman. Show the images and ask students to guess who the people are and what they are talking about. For each of the seven images that you saw earlier, here are instructions for finding them as well as some suggested questions that you can ask:

Image 1: Pause video at 01:00

- *Can you explain this image? What's going on here?* These are vinyl records. Perhaps someone is in a record shop. Or perhaps the person is at home, choosing a record to put on.
- *Whose hand is this? What sort of person do you think it belongs to?*
- *What kind of record do you think the person is going to choose?*

Image 2: Pause video at 01:30

- *So here is the owner of the hand. Let's give him a name. What shall we call him?*
- *Where do you think he is from?*
- *What do you think he does for a living?*
- *What room is he in?*
- *What is he doing?*
- *What day of the week do you think this is?*

Image 3: Pause video at 01:33

- *Where is this woman - what room is she in?*
- *What do you think she is doing?*
- *Let's give her a name. What shall we call her?*
- *What is her relationship with the man?* If students decide that the man and woman are married, ask: *How long do you think they have been married? Do you think that they are happily married?*

Image 4: Pause video at 01:40

- *The woman walks out of the kitchen. What room is she in now?* (answer: the hall or hallway)
- *What do you call this object in the foreground of the shot?* (answer: a vase)
- *She stops because she notices something about the vase. What do you think she notices?* (Possible answers are that it's in the wrong place; it's empty - there are no flowers in it; it is cracked; it's chipped.)

Image 5: Pause video at 01:47

- *Now you can see the vase. What is the problem with it?* (answer: It is chipped - there is a piece missing.)

Image 6: Pause video at 01:50

- *She says something to the man. What do you think she says?* In my experience, students will usually suggest that the woman accuses the man in some way or another. English language learners in particular will often suggest blunt accusations (e.g. *Why did you break my vase?*). Point out that there are many ways to ask him about the vase and some will be indirect accusations. For example, she might ask her questions in one of the following ways:

"Maurice, do you know anything about the vase? It's chipped."

"Have you got any idea what happened to the vase, Maurice?"

"Maurice, I thought you said that you would fix the vase?"

Image 7: Pause video at 02:00

- *What does the man reply?*

From here, ask students to consider what happens next. Ask them to complete the story in any way that they like. Students should write a script in which they provide notes to say what happens in the video, and write a dialogue between the man and the woman.

If you ask students to do this in pairs, they can later act out their dialogues in class. Once everyone has shared their stories, show students the video. When you do this, be prepared for some disappointed faces! The outcome will often divide students. Some might enjoy the unexpected and creative use of music. Others will feel cheated.

▶ **Subject Connections**

Teachers of film studies could ask students to consider how the film "Conversation Piece" was made. For example, did the actors John Henshaw and Celia Imrie work with a script? Or did they familiarize themselves with the music so that they were able to improvise mouth movements while filming?

I got in touch with director Joe Tunmer to ask him this question. Joe told me that he did actually write a script. He spent a long time creating lines for the actors that matched with the notes, intonation, and emotion of the instruments. The actors learnt the lines while listening to the jazz piece, almost as if they were learning lyrics to a song. When Joe shot the film, he did so like a music video – with the track playing in the background. You can download the script on the accompanying website (see appendix 1 for information).

▶ **Tips for English Language Teachers**

Sometimes, the words *do you think* can make all the difference when asking questions. In the absence of these words, the student can feel that they are expected to know the answer. Here are some examples:

Teacher: *So, what happens next?*
Student: *I don't know.*

If we use the words *do you think,* the question immediately becomes an invitation for speculation. Here are two ways to do it:

1. Embed the words into the question. (*What do you think happens next?*)

2. Add the words at the end of the question. (*What happens next, do you think?*)

For English language teachers, this can be an opportunity to introduce the grammar of indirect questions:

- *Where is he from?* (direct question)
- *Where do you think he is from?* (indirect question)

- *What does he do for a living?* (direct question)
- *What do you think he does for a living?* (indirect question)

- *What room is she in?* (direct question)
- *What room do you think she is in?* (indirect question)

- *What is she doing?* (direct question)
- *What do you think she is doing?* (indirect question)

- *How long have they been married?* (direct question)
- *How long do you think they have been married?* (indirect question)

Story: "The Box"

[1, 2] Aleksander is alone in a prison cell.[3] He is sitting at a desk, reading a book. On the desk, there is a matchbox. The matchbox is moving from side to side.[4] Aleksander puts his finger on it to stop it moving. He picks it up and drops it into the desk drawer. At that moment, the door behind him opens.

Adam is pushed into the cell and the door is locked behind him. Aleksander turns around. The two men greet each other. Adam tries to make conversation with his new cellmate.[5]

"What's your name? How long have you been here?"

But Aleksander isn't interested. He turns his back on Adam and continues reading his book.[6] Adam shakes his head in disbelief. He walks over to his new bed and sits down.

On the bed, there is a red wooden box.

"What's that?" asks Adam.

"Nothing", says Aleksander without turning around.

Adam puts his hand on the box.
Aleksander turns around and says: "Stop!"

"Why?"

Aleksander takes off his glasses and looks directly at Adam.

"Don't open it!"

"Why not?"

"Because you might regret it."

"I'll take my chances."

"Fine. Go ahead. Open it."

Aleksander says nothing else. He turns around and continues to read.

Slowly, Adam opens the box.[7] He can't believe what he sees: a miniature model replica of the cell that he is in, absolutely perfect in every detail. Everything is there and everything is in place: the beds, the bare walls, the small window with bars. Incredibly, there are even two tiny figures – one sitting at the desk and another on the bed.

Adam puts his hand into the box.[8]

Video: "Room 8"

The Bombay Sapphire Imagination Series is a competition in which filmmakers have to interpret and give life to a short, ambiguous script. You can download the script on the accompanying website (see appendix 1 for information). In 2013, one of the winners was a dark short film titled "Room 8" by James W. Griffiths. The film tells the story of two men in a prison cell and a mysterious box with supernatural properties. It went on to win a 2014 British Academy of Film and Television Arts (BAFTA) award.

Discussion

Let's start with some questions that you could ask as you tell the story:

1. *This is a story that takes place in a small room without much light. Can you guess what kind of room it is?*

2. *What would you expect to see in the prison cell?*

3. *Why do you think Aleksander is there? What do you think he is doing?*

4. *Why do you think the matchbox is moving?*

5. *What do you think Adam says?*

6. *So Aleksander doesn't want to talk. How do you think Adam reacts? What do you think he does next?*

7. *What do you think he sees inside the box?*

8. *What do you think happens next? Does Adam regret opening the box?*

Unlike the questions in the previous story, virtually all of these can be answered by the short film. In other words, none of them are open-ended. But as already mentioned, the purpose of the questions is not to get the "correct" answers. It is to get students thinking and interacting.

Let's look at some examples of teacher-student exchanges and consider how we can respond to students' answers to questions like these.

Example 1

Teacher: *This is a story that takes place in a small room without much light. Can you guess what kind of room it is?*
Student: *A cellar.*
Teacher: *Yes - it could be a cellar. Any other ideas? What other kind of room could it be?*
Student: *A prison cell.*
Teacher: *Yes, perhaps it is a prison cell. Any more ideas?*
Student: *An attic.*
Teacher: *Yes - it could be an attic. Let me give you a clue. There is a small window with bars. The walls are bare. And there are bunk beds. Yes - you were right. The story takes place in a prison cell.*

Rather than saying yes or no to students' suggestions, the teacher acknowledges all answers and prolongs the guessing. In other words, a student may guess "correctly" but that doesn't mean that we have to stop there.

Example 2

Teacher: *So there is a window with bars and some bunk beds. What else would you expect to see in the prison cell?*
Student: *Pictures on the wall.*
Teacher: *No - there aren't any pictures on the wall.*

No is a powerful word and can shut down conversation. And in dialogic storytelling, it should be used sparingly. People who work in improvisational theatre groups often talk about the "Yes, and..." rule. The idea is that a performer should respond positively to what the last person said and build on the idea in some way. In this case, the teacher could have taken a "Yes, and..." approach and said: *Pictures on the wall? Yes. If you had to spend time in prison, what pictures would you put on your wall?*

Example 3
Teacher: *There is a man in the room. His name is Aleksander. What do you think he is doing?*
Student: *Sleeping.*
Teacher: *No, he's not sleeping. Can anyone else guess?*

This is a bit more complicated. In order for the story to continue, it is necessary that Aleksander is sitting at his desk, reading a book. And if students don't guess that, then how can we continue? However, the solution is very simple: accept all ideas from students without saying yes or no, and after exploring possibilities, continue the story by saying *In fact, in the story, Aleksander is sitting at a desk, reading a book.*

Example 4
Teacher: *Slowly, Adam opens the box. He looks inside and he can't believe what he sees. What do you think Adam sees inside the box?*
Student: *A tortoise!*
Teacher: *Can you explain?*

Inevitably, students will give what seem to be silly answers. When one of my own students gave this answer, I thought that it sounded strange. On another day, I might not have asked for an explanation. But I am glad that I did in this case. The student in question had a pet tortoise. She explained that every year, tortoise owners have to put their pets in boxes to hibernate. She felt that for the tortoise, it was like going to prison. So here we had a prison cell within a prison cell. I always liked that.

▶ **Students as Storytellers**
Ask students to end the story in any way they like. In order to do this, they should retell it from start to finish. For English language teachers, they should incorporate any new words, phrases, or structures into their text. Once everyone has done the task, you can show them the video.

▶ **Tips for English Language Teachers**
There is a key phrase in the story that students must understand when it comes up: *a miniature model replica*. Teach this phrase to your students before you tell the story. You could type it into an image search site and explore what you see (e.g. ships in bottles, model cityscapes, retired men making model airplanes).

You could also use "The Box" to set up a role play. When you arrive at the part when Adam enters the cell, stop the story. Ask students to prepare and act out a short dialogue in which the cellmates engage in conversation for the first time.

3.3 Students as a Resource

When you are telling a story, the students themselves can provide one of the best resources that you have. As mentioned at the beginning of this chapter, questions can be invitations for students to share their own stories, experiences, and personalities. For example, if we refer to the previous story ("The Box"), we could ask:

- *Would you rather spend a year alone on a desert island or a month in prison?*

- *What kind of beds do you often find in prison cells?* (answer: bunk beds) *Does anyone here have a bunk bed? Who do you share with? Do you sleep on the top bunk or the bottom bunk?*
- *How would you feel if your new cellmate didn't want to make conversation with you?*
- *Do you think that Adam should open the box? Would you?*

Questions can also transport a student into the story and give them the role of the protagonist. One way to do this is to tell the story in the second person:

At that moment, the door behind Aleksander opens. You are thrown into the cell. The door is locked behind you. Aleksander turns around and looks at you. You greet each other. Then you try to make conversation with your new cellmate. What do you say?

As you read the following story, consider how you could apply some of these ideas in your own classroom.

Story: "Pogo and the Mystery Object"

1. Pogo Wakes Up

If I were to describe Pogo, I would use three adjectives: lazy, greedy, and curious. I would also say that Pogo is a creature of habit.[1] For example, every day at the same time, he takes an afternoon siesta in the sun.[2]

Today Pogo is taking his afternoon siesta in the sun, when suddenly...

THUD!

2. A Careless Parachutist

[3] Imagine this: You are sitting in a small plane. You are flying at an altitude of about 1,000 metres. The door of the plane is open and in a little while, you are going to jump out of it.[4]

In your hand, you are holding an object.[5]

Suddenly, the plane hits a little bit of turbulence. As a result, you drop the object and it falls out of the airplane door.
You've lost it forever.[6]

3. Pogo's Reaction
So what happened to your object? Well, it fell toward Earth and took about twenty-five seconds to land on the ground with a . . .

THUD!

The sound wakes up Pogo from his afternoon siesta in the sun. Naturally, he comes to investigate.

And how does he react to the mystery object?
Well, he tries to eat it of course. What a greedy pig!

So what was the mystery object? Well, there are many things that a careless parachutist could drop out of a plane. It could have been a pair of sunglasses, a shoe, a pocket knife, a coin, a lucky charm, an apple, a cereal bar, or a can of juice, but it wasn't.

If it had been any of those things, we would know nothing about this story. And this is a true story.

Video: "Camera Falls from Airplane and Lands in Pig Pen"
The story is based on a YouTube video that is titled "Camera Falls from Airplane and Lands in Pig Pen". Seeing the incident from the video camera's point of view, we start off in the plane and end up on the ground, looking up at the sky.

When the curious pig enters the frame, it sniffs the camera and then tries to eat it. This gives us a comical close-up view of the pig's nose and then the inside of its mouth.

The video was uploaded onto YouTube in February 2014 and by the end of the year, had been viewed approximately fifteen million times. According to the description, the video camera was found by a pig farmer eight months after it was dropped from the plane.

Discussion

Here are some example questions that you could ask as you tell this story. All of them are intended to use the students as a resource.

1. *Is there anyone here who thinks that they are a creature of habit? Why do you think that? Give us an example of one of your habits.* Sometimes, the best way to get the ball rolling is to lead by example. In this case, I tell students that my friends accuse me of being a creature of habit. Whenever we meet for coffee, I always want to go to the same café, whereas they want to try different places.

2. *Does anyone here like the idea of siestas? Do you ever take siestas? When, how often, and for how long?*

3. *Has anyone here ever done a parachute jump or do you know anyone who has done one? If I gave you the opportunity to do a parachute jump tomorrow instead of coming to school, would you say yes or no? What if I offered you money?*

4. *How do you feel? What are you thinking?*

5. *What are you holding in your hand? It could be anything – something practical or something personal.* Ask students to hold out one hand in front of them and decide what they are holding. Then ask them to write down their objects on a little piece of paper. Once everyone has done this, they should give their pieces of paper to you.

6. *Oh no! What were you holding? Why were you holding that? How do you feel about losing it?* This is key. Each piece of paper in your hand represents a possible story from a student. Go through them one by one and find out who was holding what. In each case, ask individuals to explain why they were holding their chosen objects. In my experience, the most common objects include coins, lucky charms, apples, mobile phones, photographs, tennis balls, and cigarette lighters. Interestingly, when I ask my own students how they feel about losing their objects, they usually say that they are disappointed. But no one is ever worried that their object will land on an innocent person's head. This concerns me.

From here, finish the story and ask students to guess what the real mystery object was. Finally, show them the video.

► **Tips for English Language Teachers**

"Pogo and the Mystery Object" contains a juicy conditional structure: *It could have been a* [object] *but it wasn't. If it had been a*
[object], *we would know nothing about this story*. When you reach
this part of the story, represent this structure on the board with the
following grid and gaps to fill in.

I. C. H. B. A _____ B. I. W.

I. I. H. B. A _____ W. W. K. N. A. T. S.

Go through your students' suggested objects – the ones that they
wrote on the pieces of paper. For each suggestion, recite these two
lines, for example:

*It could have been a **lucky charm** but it wasn't.*
*If it had been a **lucky charm**, we would know nothing about this*
story.
*It could have been an **apple** but it wasn't.*
*If it had been an **apple**, we would know nothing about this story.*

Eventually, ask individual students to refer to the grid to recite the
lines themselves. Then remove the grid from the board and ask
students to say the lines from memory. Note that if anyone wrote
camera or *mobile phone* on their pieces of paper, you can leave
these until the end.

3.4 Eliciting

Of course, not all questions will be open-ended. As teachers, we
sometimes want specific answers to the questions that we ask.
This is sometimes referred to as eliciting. At its simplest, eliciting
is getting students to provide information rather than providing it for them. Here are some examples of eliciting questions:

- *Can you give me an example of…?*
- *Can you explain why..?*
- *What is the opposite of…?*
- *What do you call…?*
- *What does it involve?*
- *What is the difference between…?*
- *How do you say that in English?*

There are a number of reasons for eliciting:

- It uses students' collective knowledge as a resource.
- It requires students' attention and interaction. This makes learning more memorable.
- It allows us to find out what students already know or understand.
- It provides us with a tool for revising or revisiting a subject.

As you read the following two stories, consider what eliciting questions you could ask. The first story may be of particular interest to English language teachers. The second will be useful for science teachers in particular.

Story: "Worst Best Man"

I want to tell you about a funny wedding video from YouTube
It is an amateur video and it was filmed outside
It's a perfect day
The sun is shining
There's not a cloud in the sky
Five people are standing next to a swimming pool:
Three men and two women[1]

The men are wearing dark suits
One of them is also wearing a gown
One of the women is wearing a long white dress

▶

The other is wearing a long yellow dress
And she's holding a bunch of flowers[2]
Bride and groom, bridesmaid, best man, and the priest[3]

The bride and groom are taking their vows:[4]
"To have and to hold from this day forward
For better for worse
For richer for poorer
In sickness and in health
Till death us do part"[5]

And now they need the rings[6]
The best man steps forward to present them
But as he does so, disaster strikes!
This will certainly be a day to remember

⏍ Video: "My Clumsy Best Man Ruins Our Wedding"

This story is based on a YouTube video that appears to be a clip
from an amateur wedding video. The picture is shaky and the
audio is bad. But that doesn't distract from the tragedy and
comedy of the incident that was caught on camera: the best
man accidentally slips and pushes the bride and priest into a
swimming pool.

"My Clumsy Best Man Ruins Our Wedding" was uploaded
onto YouTube in 2008. With over ten million views, it would
seem to be a user-generated video that went viral. However,
there is nothing amateurish about this video at all. The people
who appear in it are actors and the whole incident was staged.

Discussion

The story describes a number of customs that are associated
with a contemporary Christian wedding ceremony. As you ask
questions and set tasks, encourage students to compare these
with other wedding ceremony customs that they know - those
relating to their own cultural or religious background perhaps.

Before beginning the story, introduce the topic of weddings.
Put students into pairs and ask them to discuss the following
points:

- *Tell your partner about a wedding that you have attended.*

- *Do you like or dislike weddings? What do you like about them and
  what do you dislike about them?*

- *Now imagine all of the things that could go wrong at a wedding
  and make a list (e.g. a dog eats the wedding cake, the bride rips
  her dress, the invitation gives the wrong date and nobody comes).*

After taking feedback, move onto the story. As you do so,
pause to ask questions. The following suggested questions are
intended to elicit wedding-related language items.

1. *What do you think they are wearing?* If students suggest that they are wearing bikinis or swim shorts, remind them that this is a wedding! Elicit wedding-related clothes and costumes, such as suits, dresses, ties, hats, and kilts. You could also ask students to consider colours of the clothes.

2. *Can you identify the five people?* Here, you are looking for the bride and groom, the best man, the bridesmaid, and the priest. However, there may be other possibilities – if it was a gay couple's wedding, for example.

3. *What other things or people do you expect to see in the video?* This question serves to elicit more wedding-related vocabulary. Possible answers include confetti, tears, the wedding photographer, dancing, and the wedding cake.

4. *Now, this is the point at the wedding when the bride and groom take their vows. What do you say when you take your vows?* This is a concept checking question. Possible answers include: *"I do", "I will", "To have and to hold from this day forward..."*

5. *What do we need at this point?* The answer that you want here is the rings. But a word of warning: Although we know what we want to elicit, the answer might not be so obvious to students. In response to the question *What do we need at this point?* a student of mine answered: *"Fidelity".* Be prepared for unexpected answers and embrace them when you can.

6. *Who carries the rings and who wears the rings?* In this wedding, the best man carries the rings. The bride and groom will later wear the rings. In other weddings, someone else might carry the rings – for example, a pageboy (ring bearer).

From here, we can ask students to guess what happens at the end of the video. One way to manage a whole-class prediction is to give "hot and cold feedback". The hotter a student's idea, the closer it is to the actual outcome. Here is an example:

Teacher: *So, what do you think happens?*
Student: *The best man has forgotten the rings?*
Teacher: *That's a great guess. But it's quite cold. Any other ideas?*
Student: *The best man drops the rings in the swimming pool?*
Teacher: *Excellent! You're hotter. It involves the swimming pool. Perhaps the rings go in the swimming pool. I'm not sure. But that's not the important thing. Any more ideas?*
Student: *The best man pushes the groom into the swimming pool?*
Teacher: *That's good. You are getting even hotter. Did he do it by accident or did he do it on purpose?*
Student: *On purpose!*
Teacher : *I'm afraid that's colder. Sorry.*
Student: *By accident!*
Teacher: *That's better. We're hot again. The best man pushed someone into the pool. Perhaps more than one person. The question is, who did he push into the pool and how did it happen?*

Eventually, show students the video and ask them who they feel most sorry for: the bride, the priest, the best man, the bridesmaid, or the groom. Go through the list of people and ask for reasons why they should feel sorry for them. Encourage students to make up possible reasons. For example, they should feel sorry for the groom because he chose the best man against his bride's wishes.

▶ **Tips for English Language Teachers**
Another way to elicit words or phrases is to invite students to finish your sentences. For example, in this story, you could say:

- *It is a beautiful day and the sun is...* (elicit *shining* or *out*)
- *holding a bunch of...* (elicit *flowers, keys, grapes,* or *bananas*)
- *For better, for...* (elicit *worse*)
- *For richer, for...* (elicit *poorer*)
- *In sickness and in...* (elicit *health*)

▶ Students as Videotellers

YouTube is full of wedding-related videos. Many of them are "fail" videos such as this one. Ask students to choose one that they like and create a story based on it.

▶ Subject Connections

For teachers of media literacy, you can use this activity to introduce the subject of fake videos on the internet. Ask students to watch the "My Clumsy Best Man Ruins Our Wedding" video carefully and decide: *Is it real? Or was it set up (staged)?* Ask students to give reasons for their answers. Students can then go online and explore the video for themselves. It is quite easy to find out that it was intended to market an independent film titled *Chloe and Keith's Wedding*.

Teachers of cultural or religious studies can use the story to look at how wedding ceremonies vary around the world according to country, culture, and religion. The story includes an excerpt from the marriage vows. It also makes reference to many specific practices in a conventional western Christian wedding:

- The bride wears white.
- The wedding party includes a bridesmaid and a best man.
- The ceremony includes a flower bouquet. (In the video, the bridesmaid is carrying it for the bride.)
- The wedding ceremony involves an exchange of rings.
- The best man carries the rings.

Ask students to investigate a wedding ceremony of a different tradition of their choice, and find out how customs and traditions can vary.

Story: "Fun with an Electric Fence" ⚠

[1,2] Imagine this: A young inexperienced cow comes into contact with an electric fence.[3] It gets an electric shock. It learns to stay away in the future!

Later, a bird lands on the same electric fence.[4] Unlike the cow, the bird does not get a shock. For the bird, the electric fence is the same as any other fence.

So why did the cow get an electric shock but the bird did not?[5] Well, the important thing is that the cow was touching the ground but the bird was not.

In the case of the cow, the electric current passes from the wire, through the cow and into the earth. In the case of the bird, the electric current continues to pass through the wire and not through the bird.

Now imagine that you wanted to touch an electric fence without getting an electric shock.[6] Perhaps the obvious thing is to touch the wire while you jump in the air. Just make sure that you let go before you land! Another way would be to touch the wire while you are standing on some sort of insulator – a plastic chair, for example.[7,8]

Five fearless teenagers take a trip into the countryside.
They take four plastic chairs with them.
They are going to carry out an experiment.[9]

The group finds an electric fence. They place the four plastic chairs in a row, perpendicular to the electric fence.
With a teenager standing on each plastic chair, all four of them join hands to form a chain. The teenager who is closest to the electric fence holds the fence with his free hand.[10]

▶

▶ As expected, nothing happens. No one gets an electric shock.

Then the fifth teenager steps forward. He doesn't have a plastic chair. He takes off his shoes and socks so that he has bare feet.[11] This will give him the best possible contact with the ground. Rubber soles could act as insulators.

He joins the chain. He takes the hand of the teenager who is farthest from the electric fence.

What happens now?[12]

Video: "Electric Fence Experiment Ends as Expected"

This video was uploaded onto YouTube in 2012 and is titled "Electric Fence Experiment Ends as Expected". It ends comically, with the five teenagers dropping to the ground with a scream and then rolling around laughing.

Science teachers all over the world should be grateful to these Australian teenagers for making this video. It provides an invaluable resource for teaching basic principles of electricity. It also serves as a warning to teenagers everywhere: you'll probably not want to try this experiment yourself!

Discussion

As you tell the story "Fun with an Electric Fence", you can pause to ask questions which invite students to theorize and explain concepts. For the suggested questions below, answers are provided in the story.

1. Begin by drawing a picture of a fence on the board (see image below). Tell students that it isn't a normal type of fence. Ask them to guess what kind of fence it is.

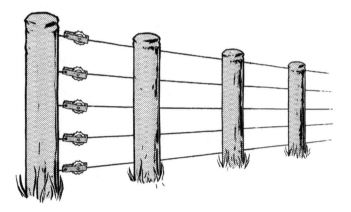

2. Once students realize that it is an electric fence, ask them to suggest places where you might find an electric fence and what purpose they serve. Electric fences can stop animals or people crossing boundaries - in other words, to keep them out or keep them in! Electric fences can be placed around high-security prisons and military bases. But most electric fences are used for agricultural purposes, for example, to stop cows leaving a field.

3. *What happens?*

4. Add to your illustration, as shown below. *What happens now?*

5. *Why did the cow get an electric shock but the bird did not?*

6. *Imagine that you wanted to touch an electric fence without getting an electric shock. What could you do?* The story describes two things that you could do. But students could give other possibilities. For example, you could touch the fence very quickly or turn off the electricity supply.

7. *Why would you not get an electric shock if you were standing on a plastic chair?* Electricity does not pass through materials like plastic, rubber, and wood. They are insulators.

8. *What is the opposite of an insulator? Can you give some examples?* The opposite of an insulator is a conductor. Conductors are materials that electricity can pass through. Metal and water are two examples.

9. *What do you think the teenagers are going to do?* After listening to students' ideas, add the plastic chairs and the teenagers to the illustration on the board, as shown.

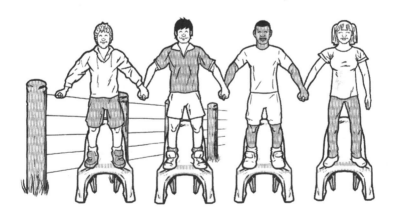

10. *What happens? Does anyone get an electric shock?*

11. *Why does the fifth teenager take off his shoes and socks? What do you think he is going to do?*

12. Add the fifth teenager to the drawing, as shown below. Ask students to predict what happens when the fifth teenager joins the chain. Many people think that only the last teenager - the one with the bare feet - will get an electric shock. This is not the case!

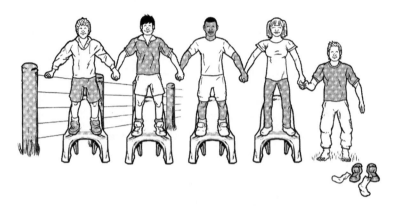

Finally tell students that the teenagers filmed the experiment and uploaded it on YouTube. Show them the video.

Appendix 3 describes an interaction technique called "Think, Pair, Share". This is a simple and effective way for students to support each other's comprehension, and could be used for many of the questions in this activity.

▶ **Subject Connections**

From here, science teachers can continue to other electricity-related concepts, such as circuits, current, AC, DC, voltage, resistance, and earthing systems.

◀ 4 ▶

Student Interaction Tasks

IN THE PREVIOUS chapter, we looked at the potential for questions from the teacher to get students thinking and speaking during a storytelling activity. In this chapter, I would like to go beyond activities where the teacher asks questions and suggest some other ways to engage students with a Videotelling story. The activities in this chapter involve a number of student interaction tasks and techniques:

- student-to-teacher questioning
- drawing
- retelling and interpreting a story
- designing a video
- collaborative filmmaking

The tasks and ideas in this chapter are versatile. You can apply them to many other stories in the book. Throughout the chapter, I will offer suggestions. Look out for the "Other Stories" headings.

All videos, materials, and resources that I refer to in this chapter can be accessed at **www.videotelling.com** For more information, see appendix 1.

4.1 Questions from Students

We have already looked at teacher questions as a way to stimulate imagination and communication. We can do the same when we encourage students to ask the questions.

Communication is a messy business. Being able to ask questions can be fundamental for clarifying, comprehending, constructing meaning, and developing ideas. It is important for any teacher to create an environment in which students feel safe to ask questions as and when they want. Storytelling provides a perfect opportunity for establishing this.

Story: "Speechless"

A woman stands in the middle of a court
She can't believe what is happening
She has her hand over her mouth
She is speechless
What is going on?

Video: "Marriage Proposal Rejected at Basketball Game"

Some people will assume that the *court* in question is a court of law. But the story is deliberately misleading. It describes an awkward moment from a viral video in which a man proposes to his girlfriend at halftime during a basketball game between the Houston Rockets and the Sacramento Kings. The video starts with the man kneeling in front of his girlfriend in the middle of the court. It ends up with the poor rejectee being consoled by Clutch the Bear, the Rockets' mascot. This is an excellent example of what young people sometimes call a "fail video".

Discussion

Start this activity by telling students that you have a puzzle for them. Read out the "Speechless" story and ask students to guess what is going on. Do not let students know that the story is based on a video. Then tell students that, in order to work out what is happening, they have to ask you questions. You can only answer yes and no. Set a limit - fifteen questions, for example.

In order to work out what is going on, students will have to consider the following:

- *What type of court is it?* (A court of law, a basketball court, a tennis court, a badminton court, or a volleyball court?)
- *What is the woman's connection with the court?* (Is she a lawyer, a defendant, a player, a cheerleader, or a spectator?)
- *Is there anyone else present?* (A judge, a witness, referees, a mascot, or her boyfriend?)
- *When does the event take place?* (Before, during or after the game, or at halftime?)
- *What is her boyfriend doing on the court?*

Once students have worked out what is going on, ask them to predict the outcome. Have a vote. *Who wants the woman to say yes and who wants her to say no?* Then show students the video.

After watching the video, ask the following questions:

- *Who do you feel most sorry for - the man or the woman? Give a reason for your answer.*
- *Do you think that either of them should have behaved differently? How?*
- *Why do some people decide to make public proposals like this? If you were going to propose to someone, how would you do it? Or if someone was going to propose to you, how would you expect it?*

▶ **Tips for English Language Teachers**

The success of this activity depends on students knowing the word *court*. You can make sure that this is the case at the beginning of the activity by typing the word into an image search site and showing students the result. Alternatively, give out dictionaries and let students find the various meanings of the word for themselves.

This activity can also provide a good opportunity to work on question forms. Take time to correct and reformulate students' questions as they ask them.

▶ **Other Stories**

Every story activity in this book involves creating an information gap between teacher and students. This means that there is always the possibility to invite questions from students. For example:

- *"Lepus arcticus"* in chapter 1: In the story, Megan notices something in the video that no one else noticed (an Arctic hare). Invite students to ask questions to guess what the thing is.
- "Jamie's All-Time Favourite TV Advertisement" in chapter 2: Ask students to ask you questions to work out what the mystery product is.
- "Worst Best Man" in chapter 3: Instead of using the "hot and cold feedback" at the end of the activity, encourage students to ask questions to work out what happens in the video when the best man steps forward.
- "Can't Hug Every Cat" in chapter 3: Students can ask you questions in order to work out how Debbie was able to upload Cara's online dating video.

Story:

"The Story of a Wannabe YouTuber and a Carolina Reaper" ⓘ

July 16, 2015: A nine-year-old schoolboy from Scotland has a YouTube channel with thirty-three videos and just eight subscribers.

July 17, 2015: The boy decides to eat a Carolina Reaper and film his reaction. When he eventually recovers from the experience, he uploads the video onto his YouTube channel.

July 19, 2015: The video has over three million views. His channel has four thousand new subscribers. His story is featured in the national and international media.

Videos: "Hottest Pepper Eaten"
and "How I Felt About Eating the Carolina Reaper"

According to *Guinness World Records*, the Carolina Reaper is the hottest chili pepper in the world. The nine-year-old Scottish boy goes by the username Pikachu the Pokemon on YouTube and his video is titled "Hottest Pepper Eaten".

In his video, Pikachu the Pokemon pops the pepper into his mouth. He chews and swallows. It takes just under a minute for the initial signs of mild discomfort to turn into the perfect image of accidental self-inflicted pain and panic.

Two days after uploading the video, Pikachu the Pokemon uploaded a second video titled "How I Felt About Eating the Carolina Reaper". In the video, he answers just about every question that we might want to ask: *Why did you do it? What happened after you turned off the camera? Where did you get the chili pepper? Would you do it again? What was it like the next day when you went to the toilet?*

Discussion

Here is one possible way of using the story and videos in class:

1. On the board, write the words: *The Story of a Wannabe YouTuber*. If necessary, explain the word "wannabe". (A "wannabe" is someone who "wants to be" famous or successful.) In this phrase, the word functions as an adjective. Find out if there are any wannabe YouTubers in your class. If so, ask them if they have a YouTube channel, how many videos they have uploaded, and how many subscribers they have.

2. To the title on the board, add the words: *and a Carolina Reaper*. It should now read: *The Story of a Wannabe YouTuber and a Carolina Reaper*. Immediately ask students to put up their hands but stay silent if they know (or think they know) what a Carolina Reaper is.

3. Invite students to work out what a Carolina Reaper is by asking you questions. Importantly, you can only answer yes or no. You can set a limit on the number of questions that students can ask (twelve, for example). You can also give the following clues to help them if and when necessary:
   - *It is in Guinness World Records. (In other words, it holds a world record.)*
   - *It is small and red.*
   - *It is something that you can eat.*

4. Once students realize that a Carolina Reaper is the hottest chili pepper in the world, ask them if they would eat one. Then give them the following question: *Imagine that you have to eat a Carolina Reaper. But you get a reward when you do it. You can either have £5000 (or $5000, €5000, etc.) or five thousand subscribers to your YouTube channel. The choice is yours. Which would you take - the money or the subscribers?* You could put students into groups to discuss this. Ask them to give reasons for their answers. Interestingly, in my

own experience, a lot of teenagers would take the subscribers over the money.

5. Tell students the story and then show the first video "Hottest Pepper Eaten". Find out who feels sorry for the boy in the video and who doesn't. Ask students to give reasons for their answers.

6. Tell students to imagine that they are going to meet the boy in the video. Tell them that they are going to interview him about his story. Ask everyone to prepare by writing down five questions that they would like to ask him.

7. Let students share their questions with you and each other. If possible, encourage them to speculate on answers. Possible questions include the following:
   - *What was it like to eat the Carolina Reaper?*
   - *Where did you get it?*
   - *What happened after you turned off the camera?*
   - *Was it as painful as it looked?*
   - *Why did you do it?*
   - *Would you do it again?*
   - *What was it like when you went to the toilet the next day?*

8. Show students the second video – "How I Felt About Eating the Carolina Reaper". Finally ask students if there is anything that we can learn from this story. Important note: It is essential that your students do not leave the room thinking that it would be a good idea to eat a Carolina Reaper or a similar chili pepper. In 2008, a British chef died, and his death was attributed to the fact that he'd consumed a pepper like this. Perhaps you should show students the article. You can access it on the accompanying website (see appendix 1 for details).

▶ **Tips for English Language Teachers**

This activity allows you to work on superlative structures. Once students know that the Carolina Reaper is in *Guinness World Records*, they will have to produce superlative structures as they make their guesses (e.g. *the oldest farmer in the world, the most expensive jewel in the world, the smallest tomatoes in the world*). Work with these and write them on the board. Alternatively, elicit the phrase *the hottest chili pepper in the world* with the letters T.H.C.P.I.T.W.

Students of English may want to know what a reaper is (i.e. a person or machine that harvests a crop). But it is the chili pepper's connection with the Grim Reaper that is more interesting. In many cultures, the Grim Reaper is the personification of death and it would seem that the Carolina Reaper is named for its deadly properties!

▶ **Subject Connections**

For science teachers who are interested in taking things further, the spicy chemical in chili peppers is called capsaicin. It probably functions as a deterrent against certain mammals and fungi. Capsaicin is also the active component in pepper spray. In the world of chili pepper cultivation, spiciness is measured in the Scoville scale. Geography teachers could connect the story to the subject of chili pepper cultivation around the world.

▶ **Students as Videotellers**

Students can look for other well-known videos in which things didn't go according to plan. There are many examples on YouTube. For example, students could investigate and tell the story of Tori Locklear. This thirteen-year-old girl decided to create an instructional video to show how to use electric hair tongs (a curling iron). In her video, Tori looks at the camera in horror when she realizes that she has burned off a lock of blond hair. Like Pikachu the Pokemon,

Tori decided to use the video to her advantage. She uploaded it onto YouTube and became a celebrity for a week. She currently has ninety thousand subscribers and continues to upload videos.

Story: "A Story of Real Estate and Death"

This story involves the following characters:
- Victor, the victim (who gets eaten alive in his own home)
- Regina, the real estate buyer (who successfully acquires Victor's property)
- the giant
- the monsters

1. Introduction
This is the story of a group of property buyers
With dangerous lives
A group of property buyers
Who spend their time making risky acquisitions
In their housing market, competition is fierce

They have to fight to get what they want

Today, there is new real estate on offer:
A small property with one bedroom
One previous owner
And a sea view

Perhaps this sounds like a nice little place to live
But this property has a dark side:
Its previous owner was murdered at home
He was eaten alive by a giant

For the property buyers in this story
The previous owner's death is not a problem
In fact, it is necessary for the acquisition

2. Victor's Story

This story takes place on a tropical beach
A beautiful place with white sand and shallow water
The tropical beach is a beautiful place
But it's also a dangerous place
It's the home of many monsters – monsters with big teeth
They hide in the deep water, waiting for the tide to go in

Today, Victor is exploring the shallow water
Victor thinks that it is safe
Because the tide is out and the monsters can't reach him
But is it?

Suddenly, the giant appears
Victor runs away
But it is too late – the giant sees Victor and starts to chase him
Victor runs as fast as he can
But the giant is too fast
Tired and exhausted, Victor tries to escape into his home
But there is no escape!

3. Regina's Story

The smell of death is carried through the sea
For Regina, this is a familiar smell

For Regina, it is essential that she has the best possible
protection from the monsters
And for this, she needs the most secure home that she can get
Regina uses the smell of death to locate the new property
And when she arrives at the scene, she looks up and sees . . .
The giant eating the last pieces of meat out of poor Victor's home

Unfortunately, Regina is not alone
In this housing market, competition is fierce
Others have arrived at the scene
They, too, used the smell of death to locate the property
They, too, need the most secure home that they can get
They, too, want the best possible protection from the monsters

They all wait nervously for the giant to finish his meal
Because when the giant finishes his meal . . .
The property will be ready for release

But Regina can't wait any longer
It is time for her to make a dangerous move
It is time for her to make a risky acquisition
She climbs up the giant
She walks in through the front door of Victor's property and . . .
She makes herself at home

The giant drops the property and it falls slowly to the ground . . .
With Regina safely inside
For Regina, this new home is more secure than her previous one
And it fits perfectly
And this is the perfect moment
Because the tide is coming in
And so are the monsters

⎕ Video: "Giant Horse Conch and Burglar Hermit Crabs"

The story is based on a video clip from the BBC nature documentary series *The Blue Planet*. In the clip, we meet a group of hermit crabs whose survival depends on acquiring shells from devoured snails. On YouTube, the video is titled "Giant Horse Conch and Burglar Hermit Crabs". In the story, Victor is a tulip snail, Regina is a hermit crab, the giant is a giant horse conch, and the monsters are sharks and rays.

The video is narrated by Sir David Attenborough who is famous for his work on British natural history documentaries. He poetically compares the hermit crabs' fight for a new shell with a competitive housing market in the human world.

Discussion

The story is intended to be confusing and ambiguous. Indeed, the ambiguity and the mysterious murder will draw many students in. Asking questions is an excellent way for them to make sense of the story and for you to check comprehension.

The story is in three parts (*Introduction*, *Victor's Story*, and *Regina's Story*). After each part, you can conduct a student-to-teacher question-and-answer session. Alternatively, invite students to interrupt you politely at any time during the story to ask a question.

For this activity, do not insist that students ask you closed questions (questions to which the answer can only be *yes* or *no*). Let students ask you anything they like. It is then your job to decide how to deal with their questions. This will require improvisation. In some cases, you may even refuse to give an answer. Here are some example questions with possible answers and comments:

Student: *Are the characters human?*
Teacher: *Good question! No, the characters in this story are not human.*

In my experience, this is one of the first questions that students will ask. Do not be disappointed when it happens. It will not ruin the surprise at the end of the story. Part of the process is for students to guess what kind of animals the characters are.

Student: *What kind of animals are they?*
Teacher: *Well, that is what you have to work out. What do you think?*

Student: *How big is the giant?*
Teacher: *The giant is huge. If Victor was the size of a football, the giant would be the size of this room.*

Student: *Does Regina know the smell because she herself has killed before?*
Teacher: *That is an interesting question. I imagine that Regina would be too small to kill Victor. But I also imagine that if she could kill Victor, she might choose to do so. She would definitely have her reasons.*

Student: *Why is the smell of death familiar to Regina?*
Teacher: *Because this is a situation that she has experienced before. It's as simple as that.*

Student: *Does the giant know that Regina and the other property buyers are there?*
Teacher: *Interesting question... Unfortunately, I really don't know the answer. Perhaps the giant knows that Regina and the other property buyers are there. Perhaps the giant doesn't care.*

Student: *Does the giant eat the home as well?*
Teacher: *No, the giant doesn't eat the home. It is made of hard material and the giant has no teeth.*

I suggest that you tell students the story at least three times. Each time they hear it, students will notice new information and think of new questions. Also, tell students that the story describes a real event that takes place on a daily basis – an everyday situation that they may or may not be familiar with. Once students have made some sort of sense of the story, show them the video.

Appendix 3 describes a technique called "Question Tokens". This is a simple way to get shy or reluctant students involved. Give out a question token to each student. (These can be pieces of card, bottle tops, buttons, plastic coins, etc.) When a student asks a question, he or she has to give the question token back to you. Everyone in the class must spend his or her token before you get to the end of the story.

► **Tips for English Language Teachers**
Activities like this one can be used to encourage students to ask questions and make requests which relate to language as well as content:

- *Can you say that last part again, please?*
- *What was that last word/phrase that you used?*
- *How would you say that in Spanish/German/etc.?*

This story contains a number of phrases that students may not know. Before telling the story, give students the groups of words below. Then ask students to predict the phrases that they will meet by matching each trio of words on the left with those on the right.

real	water
shallow	estate
fierce	competition

the previous	owner
the housing	release
ready for	market

a risky	acquisition
the tide is	buyers
property	out

This language activation task will allow you to check students' comprehension of the words and phrases before moving onto the story.

▶ Subject Connections

In science and biology classes, this activity can be used to introduce or review food web connections among different organisms. It can also be used to look at taxonomic ranks in biology: kingdom, phylum, class, family, genus, and species. You could use the animals in the video as examples. The giant horse conch can be described as follows:

- Kingdom: Animal
- Phylum: Mollusc
- Class: Gastropod (commonly referred to as slugs and snails)
- Family: Fasciolariidae (This family also includes tulip snails.)
- Genus: *Triplofusus*
- Species: *Triplofusus giganteus* (common name: Florida horse conch)

Also in science or biology classes, students can look at another behavioural phenomenon that hermit crabs display called the vacancy chain. This can happen when the hermit crabs find a new empty shell. Under the correct conditions, the hermit crabs will line up in order of size and then exchange shells all the way down the line from largest to smallest. This has been captured in another BBC clip titled "Amazing Crabs Shell Exchange".

Teachers of business studies could connect the story to the topic of real estate markets, home ownership, and property investment.

▶ **Students as Videotellers**

Students could make use of similar video clips to create their own Videotelling stories. Ask students to choose a narrated clip from a nature documentary that they like. The BBC has produced some excellent wildlife documentary series, such as *The Blue Planet, Life in the Undergrowth, The Life of Mammals, Life in Cold Blood,* and *The Life of Birds*. Many clips from these series are available on YouTube. Students could describe an example of animal behaviour in their own poetic words. Alternatively, they could use "A Story of Real Estate and Death" as inspiration for a piece of creative writing based on a nature documentary clip.

▶ **Other Stories**

The story "A World Champion" (chapter 1) is also deliberately ambiguous. Without knowing who Alex and his audience are or what's going on, students will want to make sense of things. Tell the story and invite students to interrupt you whenever they would like to ask a question. Again, these do not have to be *yes* or *no* questions. Students can ask you anything they like and you can provide answers at your own discretion.

4.2 Isolated Story Items

Story items are words or phrases from a story that refer to key things featured in the story. These can be objects, people, places, actions, events, or spoken lines. You can use these to engage students with a story before you tell it to them. For example, before telling the story "An Embarrassing Phone Call" (chapter 3), I suggested that you write the following isolated story items on the board:

- *"Answer it on loudspeaker!"*
- *an embarrassing phone call*
- *an embarrassed teacher*
- *an embarrassed student*
- *April* (the girl's name)

From here, you can ask students to refer to the story items to predict what the story is about and what happens in it.

When using this technique, the teacher's challenge is to find the best story items that will get students thinking, making connections, asking questions, constructing internal narratives, and developing theories. Sometimes, less is more: too many story items can be confusing and I very rarely use more than five.

As you read the following story, consider which story items you could isolate. Also, consider how you would use them to engage your students before you tell them the story.

The story involves a drone. And just in case you don't know (although I'm sure you do), drones are sometimes called UAVs (unmanned aerial vehicles) and can be used for a variety of purposes, including surveillance, military operations, and aerial photography and video. Among hobbyists, some popular models are called Phantoms, which are produced by the Chinese company DJI.

Story: "Zwier's New Toy"

Have you ever wondered what would happen if you were flying a drone and the battery died? Well, the DJI Phantom has a safety feature. Just before the battery dies, the drone will make an automatic landing. A Global Positioning System (GPS) inside the machine will guide it back to the same spot where it took off from. Clever, eh? What could possibly go wrong?

It's a cold day in December. A young Dutch man called Zwier goes out with a group of friends to test his new DJI Phantom.

He places it in the middle of a quiet road. It takes off and Zwier flies it above the houses, the trees, the roads, and the canals.

After about fifteen minutes, however, the battery starts to die. The drone begins its automatic landing. But instead of landing on the road, the drone slowly starts to come down above a canal. The problem is that Zwier didn't set the GPS correctly!

The canal is wide and deep. The drone is going to land right in the middle of it. Zwier has no choice. He runs to the canal and jumps in. The ice-cold water comes up to his waist.

Zwier moves to the centre of the canal as quickly as he can. He is desperate to catch the drone before it lands in the water. The water gets deeper and deeper as he goes: up to his chest, up to his neck, and then up to his chin.

The drone is just centimetres from the surface. With all his effort, Zwier throws himself forward and reaches out his arms.

So does Zwier manage to save his drone before it lands in the water?

Video: My First Day with My Drone

As you have probably guessed, the event described in the story was caught on camera. But did you guess that the camera in question is the one attached to the drone itself? Zwier Spanjer uploaded the video onto YouTube in 2015 and it quickly went viral.

From the drone's viewpoint, we see Zwier leave his group of friends and start to run toward the spot where it is going to land. When he realizes that it might land in the water, the situation becomes tense and comical at the same time.

If you want to find out whether or not Zwier saves his drone, you will have to watch the video for yourself – I don't want to spoil the surprise!

Discussion

When using this story with my own students, these are the isolated story items that I select:

- *a* DJI *Phantom*
- *a cold day in December*
- *an automatic landing*
- *a canal filled with ice-cold water*
- *a desperate man*

Here is one way to tell the story and engage students:

1. Tell students that you are going to tell them a true story but do not tell them that it is based on a YouTube video.

2. Write the isolated story items on the board. Tell students that they are things that are involved in the story.

3. Find out if anyone knows what a DJI Phantom is. If not, you can invite students to ask you questions in an attempt to work it out for themselves. You can use an image search site to show students some pictures of DJI Phantoms. And importantly, find out if anyone in the class is interested in drones and aerial photography.

4. Put students into small groups. Tell them that they are going to try to predict what happens in the story – from the beginning to the end. In order to get the ball rolling, allow your students to ask you a few questions, which you can answer at your own discretion. This should allow students to make connections between the isolated story items and address any confusion that they may have. Questions might include the following:
   - *Does the* DJI *Phantom belong to the desperate man?*
   - *Does the man fall in the canal?*
   - *Does the* DJI *Phantom make an automatic landing? Why?*

5. Once students have made guesses about what happens in the story, ask a spokesperson from each group to present their group's idea.

6. After hearing all of the groups' ideas, tell students the story "Zwier's New Toy". As you do so, pause from time to time and invite students to predict what happens next.

7. Tell students that as a result of this incident, Zwier became famous for a week. The story was shared online and featured in the mainstream media. Ask them to guess why. The answer is that the incident was caught on camera and the video went viral.

8. Before you show students the video, ask them to guess what happens at the end: *Does Zwier save his drone or does it land in the canal?*

► **Subject Connections**

For teachers of literature and psychology, this story could be used to explore *schadenfreude* – a German word that refers to the pleasure that humans can feel as a result of other people's failures. Before showing the video, find out who wants Zwier to save his drone and who wants to see him fail. In my experience, a minority of students will want to see the latter outcome. Ask those students to justify their answer and introduce them to the *schadenfreude* concept. Ask students to think of examples of TV shows and other types of entertainment that focus on other people's misfortunes.

The subject of drones may be relevant to teachers of ethics, law, and current events. It provides many issues for discussion and debate. For example: *How could drones be used for law enforcement and surveillance? How might things change in the future?*

▶ **Other Stories**

The isolated story items technique can be applied to many of the stories in this book. It was already mentioned in "Halloween Horror Story" (chapter 1), "*Lepus arcticus*" (chapter 1), and "An Embarrassing Phone Call" (chapter 3). But there are many other possibilities besides these. For example, in "Pogo and the Mystery Object" (chapter 3), give students the following list of isolated story items and invite them to ask questions or make predictions about the story before they hear it:

- *a clumsy skydiver*
- *a surprised farmer*
- *a GoPro camera*
- *fifteen million views*
- *a greedy pig*

▶ **Isolated Stills**

A similar way to engage students with a story like "Zwier's New Toy" is to make use of an isolated still like the one below. Before telling the story, show students an image and ask them to predict what happens.

4.3 Storytelling Gap Fill

We usually associate fill-in-the-gap activities with handouts and exercise books. In these examples, students work with a text that contains blanks – missing words or information. Students have to consider what the missing words could be and write them in the blanks to complete the text.

In contrast, a "storytelling gap fill" involves no paper or pens. You, as the storyteller, have the job of providing the text verbally. The students' job is to listen carefully and fill the gaps in the story whenever you pause.

To prepare for a storytelling gap fill, choose a short story and decide where the blanks will be. In other words, select a number of key words or phrases from the text. Before you tell the story to your students, write the key words or phrases on the board. In the following story, I have shown my suggestions in bold.

This story involves a crowdfunding campaign. As I am sure you are aware, crowdfunding is a way of raising money for a product or project. It usually involves a website where people can make contributions. At the time of writing, the best known websites are probably Indiegogo and Kickstarter. Most successful crowdfunding campaigns involve a video which tells the story of the project and asks people to get involved. Incidentally, the book that you are reading right now was financed through a crowdfunding campaign.

Story: "A Killer Product" 🄸

Lorenzo Maggiore is not the type of person that you would expect to run **a multimillion-dollar business**. As a young man, he was a bit of an outsider who preferred surfing to studying. He left school at an early age and this worried his parents. But Lorenzo's big sister saw potential in her brother.

▶

▶ She persuaded him to pursue **a career in art**.

As an artist, Lorenzo became obsessed with an idea – an idea that he had had since he was a child. And he was sure that if he could bring his idea to commercial life, he would have **a killer product**.

Unfortunately, Lorenzo was not known as a businessman. No bank in the world would give him **the funding that he needed**. He had to look for alternative ways to get money.

In 2013, Lorenzo launched **a crowdfunding campaign**. He introduced his killer product to the world through **a promotional video on YouTube**. The video shows the product in action and consists of **a montage of deaths**. Victims are thrown into the air. They hit walls and fall to the floor. Dead!

As a result of the crowdfunding campaign, Lorenzo managed to raise **approximately $500,000 in just two months**. In the world of internet entrepreneurialism, his story provides **an interesting case study**.

⎁ Video: "Bug-A-Salt in Action!"

Although this story may sound horrific, Lorenzo's product is not as bad as you might think. The killer product is called the Bug-A-Salt – a gun that fires table salt at flies and mosquitoes in order to kill them. It's an alternative to a fly swatter. You can see Lorenzo's campaign video on his YouTube channel (channel name: "The Bug-A-Salt"; video title: "Bug-A-Salt in Action!"). Because there are many videos on the channel with similar names, I would suggest accessing this one on the accompanying website (see appendix 1 for information).

The first twenty seconds of the video give a demonstration of how to fill the Bug-A-Salt gun with salt. For the rest of the video, we see artistic close-ups of its victims, their deaths played in slow motion. Some flies are thrown against walls and other objects. Others are thrown into the air and spin like ballet dancers before falling to the ground.

You can also see Lorenzo's crowdfunding campaign online or access it on the accompanying website.

Discussion

Without knowing that the victims in the video are flies, some people might find the story "A Killer Product" quite disturbing. Please be aware of this and be sympathetic to your students. Tell students that when they see the video, they will realize that it isn't as bad as it sounds.

Once you have told the story, ask students to speculate what Lorenzo's product could be. When you show them the video, play it from the time counter mark of 00:20. This will allow the speculation to continue, as students will only see the killer product in action. They won't actually see the Bug-A-Salt gun itself. Finally, show students the video from the beginning and also refer them to the Indiegogo campaign page.

Preparing a storytelling gap fill

To use the storytelling gap fill technique, start the activity by giving out the phrases. You can write them on the board, dictate them, or copy them onto pieces of paper and put them on the classroom walls. I usually like to leave the phrases in students' view the first time I tell the story.

Make sure that you give the phrases in random order – not in the same order as in the story. In the case of "A Killer Product", for example, the following would work:

- *approximately $500,000 in just two months*
- *a career in art*
- *a montage of deaths*
- *a promotional video on YouTube*
- *a multimillion-dollar business*
- *a crowdfunding campaign*
- *a killer product*

- *an interesting case study*
- *the funding that he needed*

Telling the story

Next, tell the story. When you do this, it is essential that you know exactly when to pause and what phrase you want your students to provide. For this reason, read directly from the text but aim to keep your eyes up as much as possible. Each time you arrive at a "gap", gesture it by putting your hand over your mouth. This will let students know that they have to fill the gap.

As you approach the gaps, pay close attention to the rise and fall of your voice. For example, consider the first sentence: *Lorenzo Maggiore is not the type of person that you would expect to run* _____ . If your tone were to fall on the word *run*, this would wrongly indicate to students that you have completed the sentence. On the other hand, if you give a neutral, level tone on the word *run*, you will demonstrate that there is more to come.

Also, be aware that in some cases, there may be more than one possible way to fill a gap. For example, the first sentence (*Lorenzo Maggiore is not the type of person that you would expect to run* _____ .) could be completed with either of the following phrases: *a multimillion-dollar business* or *a crowdfunding campaign*.

In such cases, make sure that students realize that either of these phrases could fill the gap. Entertain both ideas. You could have a vote to find out which phrase students want to complete the sentence with. Later, as the story develops, they will find out whether or not they made the correct decision. In the case of the story "A Killer Product", you may have to go through it more than once in order for students make sense of it and fill the gaps correctly.

Once you have done this, encourage students to memorize the phrases, and remove them from their view. You can then tell the story again and ask students to fill the gaps from memory.

► **Tips for English Language Teachers**

Storytelling gap fill activities can work particularly well for English language learners. As you distribute the phrases, refer to a good dictionary to teach any unknown language or concepts (*crowdfunding, a case study, a montage*). Ask students to speculate what the story is about and what happens in it.

The isolated phrases will give students an idea of what the story is about before they hear it and this can strengthen comprehension. In addition, when choosing the correct phrase to fill a gap, students have to listen carefully and think about grammar, what words go together (collocation), how ideas are organized in the text, and their different meanings.

All of this requires time to think, so don't rush the story. And importantly, in order to avoid chaos, make sure that you set down rules. Don't allow students to shout out answers. Encourage them to think carefully rather than make guesses. One way to manage a storytelling gap fill is to nominate students – in other words, call on individuals by name and ask them to give an answer.

A good follow-up for English language learners is for students to reconstruct the story text in their own words. In order to help them, give them the isolated phrases in the same order as they appear in the story:

- *a multimillion-dollar business*
- *a career in art*
- *a killer product*
- *the funding that he needed*
- *a crowdfunding campaign*
- *a promotional video on YouTube*
- *a montage of deaths*
- *approximately $500,000 in just two months*
- *an interesting case study*

There will be some flexibility here – students can use their own words to capture the meaning of the text. However, there is also some restriction: They must incorporate all of these phrases into their texts in the correct order. In language teaching, this type of activity is sometimes called "dictogloss".

▶ **Subject Connections**

For business studies classes, the world of crowdfunding is full of stories of success and failure. Some campaigns are notable for their originality. As a project task, students could find an interesting crowdfunding campaign and prepare a presentation on it.

The story also provides issues for teachers of art, ethics, and media. Although the victims in the story are flies, some people can feel quite uneasy about the violence in the video. This raises an opportunity for discussion. Flies are usually quick, annoying, and difficult to kill with your hands alone. This video slows things down and shows their vulnerability. For this reason, we may feel sympathy for them. Perhaps the video humanizes the flies. If this is the case, is it possible to create the opposite effect – to reduce feelings of compassion by dehumanizing various groups of people? Anyone who observes the media and politics will know that such nefarious practices are quite commonplace. I can recall an example from 2015 when David Cameron, the British prime minister at the time, referred to migrants attempting to reach Britain as a "swarm of people".

▶ **Other Stories**

"Zwier's New Toy" (the previous story in this chapter) would work well for a storytelling gap fill activity. I would recommend using the following phrases:

- *the battery starts to die*
- *right in the middle of it*
- *above a canal*
- *the same spot where it took off from*
- *reaches out his arms*

- *to test his new DJI Phantom*
- *up to his waist*
- *an automatic landing*
- *a safety feature*
- *before it lands in the water*

Another story that would work well as a storytelling gap fill is "Unusual Recipe" in chapter 2. After giving students a list of ingredients for spaghetti with tomato sauce, describe the preparation process. Each time you get to an ingredient, pause and let students fill the gap.

4.4 Drawing

Outside of the art classroom, drawing is often associated with younger learners. As teachers, we may feel awkward about asking teenagers or even adults to pick up their pencils and get creative. However, in my experience, drawing can work with all age groups. If you can persuade the reluctant artists to get involved, the process can be quite enjoyable and may even end in laughter.

When using stories in the classroom, we can ask students to draw scenes that are central to the narrative. This allows students to personalize the story and engage with the text at a deeper level. It also allows teachers to check comprehension of language and concepts.

For best results, I suggest that you tell students that you are not looking for elaborate works of art - just quick sketches to represent what they "see" in their mind's eye. Matchstick figures can be encouraged. You can also allow students to go high tech if they want to. As an alternative to pencils, pens, and crayons, students can use drawing applications on mobile devices.

The following story consists of a description of a single frame from a YouTube video. This makes it ideal for illustration.

Story: "Splat!"
Two young men are at work
They are sitting at a table
Gavin is on the left and Daniel is on the right
They are sitting opposite each other and they have their eyes . . .
Tightly shut[1]

There is a good reason why Gavin and Daniel have their eyes
tightly shut:
Above the table
In the space between them
There are thousands
Probably millions of . . . [2]
Pieces of red flesh, green shell, and drops of juice[3]

This is the exact moment at which . . .
The watermelon exploded![4]

To make the watermelon explode . . .
Gavin and Daniel used five hundred everyday objects[5]

 Video: "Rubber Bands Versus Watermelon"

This text is based on a video titled "Rubber Bands Versus
Watermelon". It was uploaded on YouTube in July 2012 and
has been viewed millions of times.

The video was created by Gavin Free and Daniel Gruchy,
better known as the Slow Mo Guys. The Slow Mo Guys use
high-speed cameras to film events in extreme slow motion and
share the videos on their YouTube channel. Example events
include bubbles bursting, a gun firing underwater, popcorn
popping, a collision of a football and face, and in this case, a
watermelon exploding as a result of having five hundred rubber
bands wrapped around it.

Discussion

One excellent thing about drawing is that it allows you to slow things down. It gives students time to process questions and formulate answers independently before sharing their ideas with the rest of the class. For this reason, I recommend the following format for this activity:

- Ask a question but don't let students answer it yet.
- Ask students to draw the picture and think about the question.
- Invite students to share their drawings and ideas.

For this activity, start by telling students that they are going to draw. You can reinforce this by giving out pencils and paper or by asking students to take out their mobile devices. From here, tell the story and pause to ask the following questions at the numbered points in the story:

1. *What do you think that Gavin and Daniel do for a living? And why do they have their eyes tightly shut? Before you answer that question, I want you to draw the scene as you imagine it.* After students draw, ask them to show their pictures to each other and share their theories. My own students have speculated that Gavin and Daniel are wine tasters, psychic mediums, arm wrestlers, and even civil servants. I have never had a student guess that Gavin and Daniel have their eyes closed because of an exploding watermelon. But as always, the purpose is for students to share ideas rather than guess the "correct" answer.

2. Pause here. Students will naturally want to guess how the sentence finishes. Mine sometimes guess that there are thousands and millions of flies and mosquitoes. If yours suggest this, ask them to explain where the flies and mosquitoes came from.

3. *Can you explain? Why are there thousands or millions of pieces of red flesh, green shell, and drops of juice?* For English language learners, write the words *red flesh, green shell*, and *drops of juice* on the board. At this point, these words are key to the story and it is important that students have time to comprehend them. As part of the activity, you could allow students to look for *flesh* and *shell* in a dictionary and explore the various meanings of the words before offering their explanations. One student of mine suggested that the red flesh, green shell, and drops of juice came from a turtle. I was very happy that he was wrong!

4. *So how did Gavin and Daniel cause the watermelon to explode? Before you answer that question, I want you to add the watermelon explosion to your drawings.* Although there may be many ways to make a watermelon explode, students often seem reluctant to put safety first. Suggestions from my

students have involved using explosives, dropping the fruit from a height, or bashing it with heads.

5. *Can you guess what the objects were and how they used them?* As students develop their theories, give them the extra information as clues: The five hundred objects are identical and you can buy them in an office supply shop or perhaps a stationery shop - depending on where you are in the world. Finally, show students the video.

▶ **Subject Connections**

For science and physics teachers, the watermelon video could be useful for introducing different types of energy and energy conversion. The video provides a graphic demonstration of elastic potential energy being transformed into kinetic energy.

For teachers of media or film studies, any Slow Mo Guys video could be used to introduce the principles of high-speed video cameras and techniques that are associated with them.

For business studies, students might be interested in examining how the Slow Mo Guys have become successful internet entrepreneurs. YouTube and other video-sharing sites present content creators with business opportunities and students could explore these. You could set up projects or tasks in which students do any or all of the following:

- Investigate the story behind a successful online video creator of their choice. This could be a videoblogger, a musician, an artist, or a filmmaker. Students would have to describe their work and refer to their collaborations with other video creators, film studios, or advertisers, for example.
- Find out about the YouTube partnership programme. This allows YouTubers like the Slow Mo Guys to share revenue with YouTube that is generated from advertising on their videos.
- Consider what makes a successful YouTuber/video content creator.

▶ **Other Stories**

Drawing activities could be integrated into all of the following stories:

- "A Tale of Two Ryans" (chapter 1): Before you tell the story, ask students to draw a picture, given the following description: *A man is sitting very close to his television. He is facing the screen and has a video camera in one hand and a spoonful of cereal in the other.* Then ask students to guess what is going on before moving on to the story.
- "A Story of Real Estate and Death" (this chapter): Ask students to draw the moment when Regina and the other property buyers arrive at the scene and see the giant.

4.5 Retelling and Interpreting a Story

This is one of the first writing tasks that I can recall from my childhood: The teacher would tell us a story and we would all write it up in our notebooks. Of course, we would have to accompany it with a drawing!

Usually, when we choose to retell and interpret, we have a good reason for doing so. We might choose to tell a friend about an advertisement that we saw on TV simply because we like it. Or perhaps we found it funny, stupid, or inappropriate. In short, there is no retelling without some level of comprehension, some personal response, and some interpretation.

Story: "The Woman with the Big Heart"

I want to tell you a story but first let me ask you a question:

Do you ever smile at strangers?

Where would you do this and what does it depend on?

▶

This is the story of the woman with the big heart
No matter where she is or what she is doing
The woman with the big heart smiles at everyone
Without discrimination

Can you imagine what it would be like to smile at everyone you see?
Can you imagine the benefits?
Can you imagine the problems?

Perhaps the world needs people like the woman with the big heart
Smiles spread happiness
They make us feel good
Unfortunately, for the woman with the big heart...
Her big heart is also her burden

The woman with the big heart is alone in the big city
And in the big city, smiles can give the wrong impression
Big hearts can get hurt

And the biggest problem for the woman with the big heart is this:
Nobody smiles back
And each time this happens . . .
Her heart gets a little bit smaller

The woman with the big heart has had enough
Her heart has never been smaller
Sad and lonely, she is starting to lose her smiles and find frowns

But then, from out of nowhere . . .
A friendly face appears
The friendly face stops and says . . .
"Hello!"

With a heart that is small, but not quite broken, the woman says
hello back

"Do you need help?"

"Who doesn't?"

"Is that your heart?"

"Yeah."

"It's big!"

"It's small now."

"Small?"

"It was bigger before."

"Scary!"

"Yeah – that's my problem."

"Do you want to get a cup of coffee?"

"Now?"

"Yeah. Now."

> "Okay."
>
> Happiness can depend on other people
> And after a few days, the woman's heart is back to its normal size
> Her frowns have gone and her smiles have come back
> Once again, she is the woman with the big heart
>
> And although that is not the end of the story, that is where we are going to leave it for the moment
>
> So, how would you like the story to finish?
> Will you give it a happy or a sad ending?

Video: "Another Chance"

The story "The Woman with the Big Heart" is based on the narrative of a music video for DJ Roger Sanchez's "Another Chance". The video was written and directed by Philippe André.

In the video, André uses a simple yet effective device. He takes a standard metaphor - that of a big heart as a symbol of openness - and represents it literally on the screen. In the video, we see the woman carrying a giant red heart around the streets of New York City. Of course, students probably won't realize that this is to be taken literally when they hear the story.

Discussion

After telling the story to students, give them time to share their ideas about how the story should end. After that, tell them that it is based on a music video and show them Roger Sanchez's "Another Chance".

In my experience, the video will divide people. Some feel that it has a positive message and others see it as being quite negative. Find out what your students think and ask them to give reasons for their answers. Here are some of the ideas that some of my own students have offered:

- *"Regardless of the man's behaviour, the story has a happy ending for the woman. After all, she has found her smiles again."*
- *"The woman is trapped in a never-ending emotional cycle that pushes her from one extreme to the other. How can that be good?"*
- *"It is very sad that we find it difficult to handle people who are so open."*
- *"The woman is deluded. Everyone knows that it would be a terrible idea to smile at everyone you see. The woman had to learn a lesson."*

Sometimes, it takes time for opinions to form. For this reason, you could ask students to retell and interpret the story of the video as a homework assignment. Give students access to the music video, and ask them to retell it in their own words and give their own interpretations.

Finally, two warnings: First of all, when you ask students to retell a story, some students might change details and events. Some students might even create a different story based on a similar theme. For example, one student of mine handed in a written assignment titled "The Man with the Big Liver". Establish the rules before setting the task. Secondly, don't ever assume that everyone will like the stories that you choose and tell. Be prepared for some students to use an extended task as an opportunity to tell you how much they hated it. This is perfectly valid and if it hurts your feelings, you'll just have to accept it (as I did).

▶ **Tips for English Language Teachers**

In order to retell a story, English language learners will need a lot more support. You can anticipate unknown or problematic words and phrases from the story that will be key to retelling it (e.g. *to give the wrong impression, to get a little bit smaller, to frown, a burden*). Introduce these to your students before you tell the story, write them on the board and ask students to copy them into their books. Tell the story from beginning to end more than once. Later, when students retell the story, they should incorporate these language items into their texts (spoken or written).

▶ **Other Stories**

There are many other stories that can be retold and interpreted in this book. Unlike this one, however, most of them will work best before students see the video. These include:

- "Always Misunderstood" (chapter 1)
- "Lambs to the Slaughter" (chapter 2)
- "The Story of David and Matthew" (chapter 3)
- "Can't Hug Every Cat" (chapter 3)
- "The Box" (chapter 3)
- "A Story of Real Estate and Death" (this chapter)

4.6 Designing a Video

Creating even the simplest video requires creative planning and problem solving. As teachers, we can look for ways to put students into the roles required of a video production team. We can set up tasks that require them to develop stories, communicate effectively, collaborate, consider design issues, and solve problems.

The following story and task illustrate the potential for students to design videos. Note that this task focuses on students *designing* a video. For teachers who would like to go further with the process and get students to create videos, please see the next section, Collaborative Filmmaking, and appendices 4 and 5.

Story: "OMG! WTH?"

Right, so I'm walking in the street
And this woman stops me
She's got a problem
Her car's broken down
She needs to go for help
She asks me to watch her car for five minutes
So I say: "No problem"
You'd do the same

Anyway, she's only been gone for about thirty seconds
When this thing . . .
This thing falls out of the sky!
This big, round metal object
It whistles through the air and . . .
Bam!
It lands right on the front of her car
The alarm goes off and there's smoke coming out of the engine

Oh my god!
What the hell is it?
I'm no expert but I think . . .
It's some kind of satellite

Anyway, the next thing – and you're not going to believe this . . .
This big black van with one-way glass – you know the kind where they can see out but you can't see in?
This big black van pulls up
And out get these guys – these big guys, huge guys
And they're wearing dark suits and sunglasses, and earpieces
You know that film – what's it called?
The Matrix? Men in Black?
Well, that's the sort of thing I'm talking about

Anyway, they get out of the van, these huge guys
They walk over to the car
The one that I'm supposed to be looking after
And they lift the satellite – or whatever it is –
Off the crumpled bonnet (hood) of the car
And they put it into the back of their big black Secret Service van
And then, the biggest one turns to me
And does this [put your finger to your lips]
As if to say: "You haven't seen a thing.
Don't tell anyone about this!"
And then they drive away

And then the woman comes back
And she says: "What the hell have you done to my car?"
So what do I say?

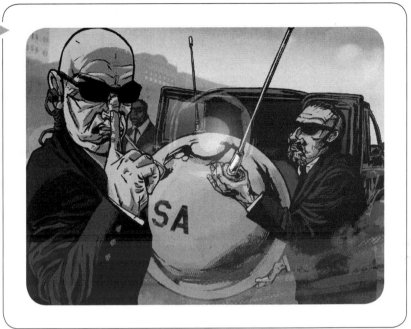

📺 Video: "NASA Satellite Falls on Car"

The story is based on a prank video. It is told from the point of view of the person who is pranked - the victim. The video was produced by *Just for Laughs Gags*, a Canadian TV show that produces content that is popular on YouTube.

Discussion

I like to use this story in class to set up a task in which students design a video. Here is how I do it:

1. Learn the story "OMG! WTH?" so that you can tell it to your students from memory. It doesn't have to be word perfect, of course.

2. Tell students the story as soon as you walk into class. Pretend that it is something that really just happened to you. I have

tried this a few times, and although I have given some Oscar-worthy performances, I have never managed to fool my students. Of course, that is not a problem. But importantly, do not let students know that the story is based on an actual video.

3. Ask students if they can describe what a prank video is (i.e. a video in which people play a trick or a practical joke on someone). Ask students if they can describe any good prank videos that they have seen online.

4. Introduce students to the *Just for Laughs Gags* YouTube channel and show them one or two examples of their prank videos. But importantly: do not show them the video "NASA Satellite Falls on Car".

5. Tell students that you have an idea. Tell them that you want them to design a prank video based on your satellite story. Ask students if they think that this would be possible. After hearing their ideas, insist that it is possible!

6. Give out copies of the worksheet on page 177. I would also suggest that you give out copies of the story "OMG! WTH?" so that students can refer it as they do the task.

7. Go over the instructions provided on the worksheet. As part of the task, students have to create a list of things that they need to make the video. Give them a few examples to get them started - for example, *some hidden cameras, an actor to play the car owner*, and *a big black van with one-way glass*.

8. Put students into teams of three or four and ask them to complete the list on the worksheet. Taking the role of the manager of the production company, you have to circulate between the different teams. Make sure that they understand the task and listen to their initial ideas.

At first, students may think that the task is easy. It can take time for them to appreciate the problem. There are two common things that students will do. The first is to add the word *satellite* to their lists. Of course, getting a real satellite would not be possible so this is not an option. Second, and more importantly, students will often assume that an object has to be dropped onto the car from a height, often using a crane, a drone, a person hiding in a tree, or even a cannon. As well as being very dangerous, this approach would not work - the object would most likely fall off the car bonnet. You could demonstrate this by dropping a dried pea onto a matchbox.

9. It is time for you (as the manager) to call everyone back for a quick meeting. Ask for everyone's attention and mention the above problems to your students. You can say something like: OK *everyone. We have a few problems here. First of all, some people want to use a real satellite. Do you honestly think that we could get a real satellite for this? No, of course not! Secondly, some people are talking about actually dropping an object from a height. Would this be a good idea? Absolutely not! This is not practical. Also, it could be very dangerous. It could kill someone. And if that happens, it will be me - the boss - who gets into trouble.*

10. At this stage, things can start to get interesting. With a bit of help from you, students should realize that success will probably involve creating the illusion of a satellite falling on the car. This could be achieved by distracting the victim of the prank in some way or another. From here, students will have to decide what the distraction is going to be and what will happen while the prank victim is distracted. (For example, some teams will decide to use two cars which can be switched during the distraction.)

At this point, students should be close to completing the list of items they will need to shoot the video. A sample list might look something like this:

- several hidden cameras
- an actor to play the car owner (the woman who goes to get help)
- a prank victim
- three actors dressed as secret service agents
- a big black van with one-way glass
- a papier mâché or polystyrene satellite, painted silver
- a smoke machine
- a remote-controlled stereo with loudspeaker to provide the sound effects
- a car
- a second car with a crumpled bonnet and the false satellite on top of it
- crew members to change the cars when the victim has been distracted

11. Once all the groups have a basic idea of how they could create such a video, ask a spokesperson from each team to present their team's idea to the rest of the class. The spokespeople should describe in detail how their team intends to create the illusion of a falling satellite and turn it into a prank.

12. After each group has presented its idea, show students the satellite prank video.

▶ Videotelling Worksheet: Plan a Video

You are part of a creative team that works for the video production company Just for Laughs Gags. Your job is to plan prank videos.

Today, you have a task. You have to plan a prank video that makes use of the satellite story. In other words, the victim of the prank should think that:

- A satellite falls out of the sky and lands on a car that he or she is looking after.
- The satellite is removed by some secret agents.

Start by deciding exactly what you need to make the video. Consider the equipment, props, and people. Make a list:

1 ....

2 ....

3 ....

4 ....

5 ....

6 ....

7 ....

8 ....

9 ....

10 ....

11 ....

12 ....

13 ....

14 ....

15

▶ Students as Videotellers

As a follow-up task, ask students to go online and choose a prank video that they like. They should then create a story in which they describe the prank from the pranked victim's point of view. The story should be in the first person.

▶ Subject Connections

For film and media studies, you could also ask students to decide whether or not they should use actors to play the parts of the pranked victims. Ask them to consider advantages, disadvantages, and ethics. Ask students to watch the video again and pay close attention to the prank victims' reactions. Are they actors or are they really members of the public? It is difficult to say. But what we do know is that a number of pranked individuals have appeared in more than one prank video. (There are a few videos online which expose this and you can access them on the accompanying website – see appendix 1 for more information.) This would suggest that at least some of them are played by actors.

▶ Tips for English Language Teachers

For English language learners, you can use the satellite story text ("OMG! WTH?") to draw attention to language features that are common when we tell anecdotes:

- present tense narrative in a story that happened in the past (For example: *This thing falls out of the sky!*)
- connecting words such as *anyway* and *well*
- the demonstrative adjectives *this* and *these* to introduce people and things into the story (*Anyway, she's only been gone for about thirty seconds when this thing falls out of the sky.*)

You could also use this story to teach certain phrases that are associated with cars (*break down, pull up, drive away, the car bonnet/the hood of the car, the front of the car, the back of the van, smoke coming out of the engine, one-way glass).*

4.7 Collaborative Filmmaking

Many of the tasks in this chapter allow students to develop, express, and share their internal narratives. In other words, they share their interpretations of the stories that they hear and the videos that they watch.

Given the nature of this book, it would seem natural to suggest tasks in which students bring their ideas to life by creating short films or videos. Filmmaking is naturally and necessarily collaborative. It requires students to work together for scripting, choosing actors, finding locations and props, directing, filming, editing, and much more. In the following activity, students work together to interpret a text and decide exactly how they are going to use it for the basis of a short film. Note that appendices 4 and 5 provide additional support for setting up and managing video-creation tasks such as this.

Story: "Left on the Shelf"

This is a story of love at first sight
And marriage at first opportunity

It's almost as if they were made for each other
Love at first sight
He was going one way
She was going the other
He smiled at her
She smiled back
And that was it . . .
No chance to stop

Neither of them thought . . .
That they would ever meet again
But perhaps this love was meant to be
Because against the odds
Their paths crossed
Not once, not twice, but three more times

They fell in love
He popped the question
She said yes
They tied the knot
And their love went from strength to strength

But then one day, everything changed
A careless little action
A situation beyond their control
And against their will, they were forced apart
Made to go their separate ways

She went on to new things
A new life
A new reason
A new purpose

But not so far away from here
In a forgotten little corner
He lives alone with nothing but memories
Loveless
Homeless
Purposeless
With a terrible feeling of emptiness
Sometimes he thinks that life might have been better
If only he had been . . .
Left on the shelf

📺 Video: "Love Story in Milk"

The story "Left on the Shelf" is based on a 2011 Friends of the Earth campaign video titled "Love Story in Milk". The video tells the sad story of two cartons of milk that fall in love but are tragically separated when one is recycled and the other is not. At the end of the video, we are told: "If you'd love to see a happier ending, tell the government you want less rubbish and more recycling."

It is especially important to realize here that the Friends of the Earth campaign video is of secondary importance to the ideas that students have and the videos that they create. I have even used the story in the past without telling students that it is based on a video.

Discussion

The story "Left on the Shelf" is intentionally ambiguous. In writing it, I have avoided reference to the *who*, *where*, *when*, *why*, and *how* facts and details. In this sense, the story provides nothing more than a framework. Students' task is to invent the missing information and turn the story into a short film. Here is one way you can do it:

1. Tell students that they are going to hear a story called "Left on the Shelf". Ask students what they think of when they hear those words. *What pictures do they imagine? A lonely book on a bookshelf? An unhappy teddy bear in a bedroom? A solitary box of cereal in a kitchen cupboard?*

2. If necessary, explain the traditional meaning of the phrase. *Left on the shelf* is quite an old-fashioned expression. If you are *left on the shelf*, you miss the opportunity to get married. Supposedly, no one wants to be left on the shelf. In that sense, it has a negative meaning. It is also sexist – it is usually used to refer to women.

3. Tell the "Left on the Shelf" story to your students. You can tell it two or three times.

4. Give out copies of the story text – one for each student. Put your students into groups and ask them to write a list of questions that relate to it – for example: *Who is he and who is she?*

5. Ask groups to share and compare the questions that they have written. Write a consolidated list on the board. If necessary, add suggestions of your own. The list may look like the following:
   - *Who is he?*
   - *Who is she?*
   - *Where are they from?*

- *Are they human?*
- *Where were they when they first saw each other?*
- *Why didn't they stop?*
- *How and where did their paths cross again (three more times)?*
- *What was the careless little action and who was responsible for it?*
- *Why did the careless little action force them apart against their will?*
- *What happened to her? What was her new life, her new purpose, her new reason?*
- *What happened to him? Why did he end up loveless, homeless, and purposeless?*
- *What can we learn from this story?*

6. Ask each group to work together to develop their own imaginative answers to these questions. As they work, the groups should develop more structured stories.

7. Finally, as a main task, each group should work together to turn their stories into short films. In order to do this, each group will have to do the following:
   - decide on a genre (drama, comedy sketch, spoof documentary, etc.)
   - create a script including a dialogue and descriptions of key actions
   - prepare costumes and props
   - decide who will play what roles
   - choose shooting locations
   - shoot the video
   - edit the video
   - share the video

If possible, I would recommend that students work together to create their films outside of school time. If this is not possible, look for quiet places for them to shoot (empty rooms in the school, a playground, a trip to the park, etc.).

Once all the groups have created and shared their work, have a class viewing. You can award prizes for the best film. Once you have done this, you can tell students that you also have a story for them. At this stage, show the Friends of the Earth video "Love Story in Milk".

▶ Subject Connections

For classes on environmental studies and citizenship, you can use the video to set up a project or discussion on recycling. For classes in drama and literature, you could use the story as a way to introduce the familiar theme of love gained and lost.

▶ Other Stories

- "Always Misunderstood" (chapter 1): This ambiguous story could be used in a similar way. Ask students to write questions about the story and then create their own imaginative answers. They can then turn their stories into short films.
- "Why Are You Lying on the Pavement?" (chapter 2): Students can act out this story and film their performances.
- "The Box" (chapter 3): This story is based on a short film titled "Room 8". The film was one of five winners in the Bombay Sapphire Imagination Series. In the competition, filmmakers interpret a short, ambiguous script and turn it into a short film. You can download the script and set this same task for your students. (You can access it on the accompanying website – see appendix 1 for information.) Once you have viewed your students' films, you can show them the five official winners in the series. They are all on the Bombay Sapphire YouTube channel.

◄ 5 ►

Media Literacy and Critical Thinking

ELCOME TO CHAPTER 5. I'm glad you got here! Throughout this book, we have seen many stories and activities in which we deconstruct videos and ask students to consider questions, such as the following:

- *Who created these videos and why?* ("Ryan Gosling Won't Eat His Cereal" series in chapter 1)
- *Is this video ethical?* ("Super Chill Monkey Does Hollywood" in chapter 2)
- *What genre does this video belong to?* ("Beans" in chapter 2)
- *Why do you think this video was so popular?* ("eHarmony Video Bio" in chapter 3)
- *Is this video real or fake?* ("My Clumsy Best Man Ruins My Wedding" in chapter 3)
- *What motivates people to create videos like this?* ("How I Felt About Eating the Carolina Reaper" in chapter 4)

Questions such as these require students to take a more critical approach to the videos that many of them watch on a daily basis. And that is the point. As educators, we need to encourage students to question the ideas and information that they encounter.

The subjects of media literacy and media education have been defined and explored over decades. Rather than examine those subjects in detail here, I will focus on three key media literacy and media education goals for teachers and students: analyze, evaluate, and create. This final chapter deals with the analysis and evaluation of online video. Throughout the chapter, I have four different but often related aims. These are to raise students' awareness of the following key issues:

- The tricks of the trade: What are the techniques and conventions that video creators use to tell their stories and elicit responses from the viewer?
- Authenticity and bias: The video tells a story, but does it do so truthfully and does it portray people and events fairly?
- Motivations: Who creates the video and with what purpose?
- Internal narratives: As mentioned throughout the book, different people will experience a story or video in different ways. But how diverse can interpretations be?

So that's the analysis and evaluation part. But what about creation? Well, if we want to train students to be truly critical, we have to get them making videos of their own. After all, you can spend a lifetime watching TV but that doesn't mean that you know how a television show is made. By creating videos, we can increase our awareness and appreciation of the ones that we see on screen. We can also develop our analytical and evaluative skills. For this reason, I would always encourage teachers to get their students involved in video creation activities. Appendix 4 offers practical and technical advice for teachers who are interested in doing so.

All videos, materials, and resources that I refer to in this chapter can be accessed at **www.videotelling.com** For more information, see appendix 1.

5.1 Sound and Vision

Video is sometimes referred to as a multimodal medium. This means that meaning is created and delivered through a combination of many different things, including moving images, graphics, onscreen text, music, sound effects, and editing techniques. In this respect, even the simplest of videos can be incredibly complex.

In this section, we are going to reduce things to just two components: the audio and visual. We are all aware that filmmakers use music to influence or enhance our mood or interpretation. For example, we might expect to hear slow violins during a sad scene or a fast-paced piece of music to accompany a car chase.

It can be easy to take conventions like these for granted. But when conventions are challenged, we might just see things in a different way. This first story is based on a video that does that.

Story: "A Gentle Giant?"

A gentle giant
Moving slowly through the blue
As calm and peaceful as the heavens above
And the green below

But don't be fooled:
I am, in fact, a demon
A fiery monster
Who hisses like a snake
And roars like a lion

So what am I?

☐ Video: "Hot Air Balloon PSA"

Although this story could refer to many things, it was inspired by a YouTube video by user WavePunk. The video is titled "Hot Air Balloon PSA" and uses a simple soundtrack to communicate a simple idea. It is very important to make sure that your volume is not too high when you view this video or when you play it in class.

The video starts with some footage of a hot air balloon accompanied by a blend of serene piano music and soothing synthesizer strings. This calm music lasts for approximately fifteen seconds. But suddenly, the hot air balloon's pilot opens the blast valve and a long flame shoots into the belly of the balloon. At that moment, the calm soundtrack is replaced by noisy heavy metal music. For the rest of the video, the audio track alternates between these two types of music. The result is that the balloon is portrayed both as a gentle giant and as a fiery monster. When the balloon disappears into the sunset, the video fades to black and a text on the black background reads: "One in five balloons feel misunderstood. Take time to talk to a balloon today." Apparently, the "PSA" in the title of the video stands for public service announcement.

Public service announcements (also called "public service ads" or "public information films") are messages which are traditionally broadcast in movie theatres or on television. They are aimed at raising public awareness of social issues, such as how to prevent the spread of disease or the dangers of drinking and driving. Despite the title of the video used in this activity, it is not a real public service announcement - it is a spoof.

Discussion

Most of the activities in this book begin with the story. But in this case, I suggest starting with the audio of the video. You can let students hear the video without seeing the images. Here is one way to structure the activity:

1. Tell students that they are going to hear two short musical excerpts. Ask students to listen to the excerpts and write down the first thing that comes to mind in each case. In other words, what does the music make them think of? What feelings does the music suggest to them?

2. Play the first thirty seconds of the video so that students can hear both the calm music (00:00-00:16) and the contrasting heavy metal music (00:16-00:30) but they can't see the video. (Important: do not play it too loud!)

3. Replay the musical excerpts again, if necessary.

4. Ask students to share their responses with each other and then with the rest of the class. Ideas from my own students have included, for part one (00:00-00:16): *nature, heaven, swans on a lake, a relaxing journey, family reunification,* and *space exploration,* and for part two (00:16-00:30): *hell, fire, a heavy metal concert, darkness,* and *death.*

5. Tell students the short story "A Gentle Giant?" and end with the words: *So what am I?*

6. Ask students to share their answers. Note that the story could refer to a number of different things - all of which are valid and can be explored. These include the wind, a whale, a cloud, or an airplane.

7. Tell students that the story "A Gentle Giant?" is based on a YouTube video. Tell them that the music that they heard is from the video. Ask students to suggest what they will see when you show them the video.

8. Show students the video "Hot Air Balloon PSA" but stop it at 01:15 - just before the final message: "One in five balloons feel misunderstood..." Ask students to discuss the following questions:

- *What do you think of this video? For example, do you think that it is funny, silly, or clever? Give a reason for your answer.*
- *What effect or effects does the music create? How does it contribute to the video? Can you put this into words?*
- *Do you think that the video creator has a message? What do you think the videomaker is wanting to communicate? Explain your answer.*

9. Show students the whole video so that they see the message ("One in five balloons feel misunderstood. Take time to talk to a balloon today."). Tell students that this video is a spoof public service announcement.

There are many standard associations between certain types of music and emotions, subjects, and ideas. Conventions like these are easy to take for granted and the hot air balloon video may challenge them. Put this idea to your students. For example, ask them to think of different animals and music that we might associate with them. There are many composers who have been inspired by the animal kingdom (for example, Rimsky-Korsakov's *Flight of the Bumblebee*; Prokofiev's *Peter and the Wolf*; John Williams's theme for the film *Jaws*, about a great white shark). You could play some of these to your students, ask them to guess the animals and discuss how objective or subjective the depictions are. In some cases, music can serve to imitate the sounds that an animal makes. But in other cases, associations will be cultural and arbitrary.

As a follow-up task, ask students to keep a journal. Over a week or so, students should pay very close attention to the films, advertisements, trailers, and videos that they see on screen. Ask them to identify, describe, and analyze five ways in which music or sound is used to set up expectations, manipulate emotions, or contribute to meaning.

► **Subject Connections**

This activity may be of particular interest to teachers of art, media, and music. For teachers of language arts, see the "audio first" idea below.

► **Audio First**

With the story "A Gentle Giant?" we saw an example of an "audio first" technique: Students heard the video "Hot Air Balloon PSA" without seeing it. This idea can work well for engaging students with a number of other stories and videos in the book. For example, before telling "The Story of David and Matthew" (chapter 3), you could let students hear, but not see, the short video that it is based on ("Blind Luck") and ask them to guess what is going on. The film has a sparse audio track which includes the following sounds:

- ding-a-ling
- footsteps
- *"Matthew?"*
- *"David."*
- coins jingling
- slow footsteps
- scratching
- ka-ching!
- *"Better luck next time."*
- *"Oh well!"*
- the sound of a card pulled across the counter and being torn up
- slow footsteps
- ding-a-ling

With one exception, all of these sounds happen as a direct consequence of actions and events in the story. For example, when David opens the shop door, a bell actually rings (*ding-a-ling*), and when he moves across the shop, this creates the sound of footsteps. But the *ka-ching* sound is different. Literally, *ka-ching* is the sound of an old-fashioned cash register. Metaphorically, however, it represents the idea of someone seeing a money-making opportunity, and that is exactly what happens in the short film.

We are quite used to representing intangible ideas with visual signs and symbols (for example, doves for peace, hearts for love, a light bulb above a head to represent an idea). But perhaps we are less aware that intangible ideas can also be represented by sounds. This is something that you can explore with your students.

5.2 Stereotypes and Identity

In the previous story, we met a hot air balloon that felt "misunderstood". Although the video was probably created for fun, it raises an important issue: What if, instead of objects, it is groups of people who are misunderstood and misrepresented in the media?

As a society, our media diet will influence us and contribute toward the way that we think about certain groups of people. Simplistic depictions lead to complex problems and this is an important subject for anyone who teaches media, film studies, citizenship, or sociology.

Story: "A Man with a Passion"
[1] Ever since he was a young boy, Tommy Carroll has had a passion . . .
A passion that requires commitment, patience, and skill[2]

Some people would describe Tommy's passion as an extreme sport
Others would say that it is a recreational activity
For Tommy, it is a way of life[3]

Always in search of the next adrenaline rush Tommy pushes himself to the limit[4]

▶

> He gets up early every day and goes to the skatepark[5,6]
> There he practises and performs ramp and lip tricks:
> Nose pivots, heel reverts, axle stalls, and more
>
> For any skateboarder, falling is a part of the sport
> According to Tommy, knowing how to fall is a skill in itself
> Something that you have to get good at
> And protective gear makes all the difference
>
> In 2013, Eyeforce, a video production company that specializes
> in extreme sports, made a short documentary film about Tommy.
> In the film, they followed Tommy to the skatepark and captured
> his skills on camera. They also interviewed him about his life, his
> passion, and his philosophy.[7]

Video: "Brave"

The short film is called "Brave" and can be seen on Vimeo. It was directed by Arthur Neumeier and is accompanied by a poignant piece of music - a song called "Where the Heart Is", which was written especially for the production.

The short film introduces us to Tommy Carroll - a skateboarder who has been blind since the age of two. Together with the story "A Man with a Passion", the short film provides material for a discussion about how people with disabilities are represented in the media.

Discussion

For many people, this short film will have a lot of appeal. Indeed, the comments left underneath the video include adjectives like *inspiring*, *stunning*, and *moving*. The film was also featured on the Vimeo website's "Staff Picks" page as one of their favourites. Students who play or watch sports may find it appealing, and many students will be familiar with the conventions of the "human interest story".

But personally – and I stress that this is my own opinion – I feel that the filmmakers have fallen into a common trap. Tommy's blindness is, without doubt, an essential part of his story. But without intending to do so, the filmmakers have portrayed him as a blind skateboarder rather than a skateboarder who is blind. They have done this in two ways:

1. The music: The producers of the film, Eyeforce, make a lot of extreme sports videos. In general, the music that they choose to accompany these films has a pace, energy, and tension that matches the sport. In the case of the video about Tommy, however, they made use of a poignant and moving ballad. This pushes us to feel sympathy for Tommy, whether we want to or not. This is a classic stereotype: to portray the person with a disability as an object of pity.

2. The title: Bravery is subjective. Different people require different levels of courage to do different things. We should not assume that Tommy is more or less courageous than the other people who feature in Eyeforce's other videos. As a title for the short film, "Brave" is obvious and unimaginative. It leads to another reductionist representation: the stereotype of people with disabilities as being inspirational heroes.

In an interview with US literary journal *McSweeney's*, Tommy himself said: "I always felt pressure to try to be the very best at any given skate park because, if I was only 'good', people would judge me as just being great for a blind skater. I wanted to be a great skater, period." You can access the interview on the accompanying website (see appendix 1 for information). It seems that Tommy doesn't define himself by his blindness. Can we say that the filmmakers approached their subject with the same openness?

But perhaps I am being unfair. If Tommy's story was not framed in this way, I am quite sure that the video would not have been as popular as it was. The media exists to give us the stories that we want and, in this respect, it reflects who we are and how we see the world.

▶ **Promoting Critical Thinking: an Approach and a Warning**

Whether or not you agree with my opinions here, I hope that you will consider that these issues are worth exploring in your classroom. When promoting critical thinking activities, it is not the teacher's role to tell students what to think. Our task is to set up conditions and ask questions which will require students to think for themselves, express themselves clearly, give support for their ideas, and listen to the opinions of others. In managing a discussion, you may want to ask students to examine their assumptions and challenge them to support their assertions; share your own opinion, but not in a heavy-handed way; play devil's advocate in an attempt to spark a debate or take a conversation in new directions.

This subject deals with blindness in particular, and disability and difference in general. Please be aware that these are potentially sensitive subjects. You may have students with disabilities who could feel marginalized by a discussion like this. And bear in mind that many disabilities are invisible. Never make assumptions. Since you can never be sure exactly what is happening in your students' lives with their friends and family members, be sensitive, tactful, and not too provocative.

To start this activity, tell students the story "A Man with a Passion" but do not tell them that Tommy is blind. Pause to ask the following questions and set the following tasks:

1. *Is there anyone in the class who would say that they have a true passion? Tell us about it.*

2. 3. and 4. At each of these moments, pause to ask students to guess what Tommy's passion is and consider ideas without telling students whether they are right or wrong.

5. After mentioning the skatepark, confirm that Tommy is a skateboarder (or a skater). Find out if you have any skateboarders in your class. If so, find out how good they are and what tricks they can do.

6. *So we already said that skateboarding requires commitment, patience, and skill. Can you think of any other things that it requires?* Take ideas from students and write them on the board. These may include good balance, strength, protective gear, knowing how to fall, and — of course — bravery or courage.

7. *So I am going to show you the video in a moment. But before I show it to you, I want you to predict two things: the kind of music you expect to hear and the film's title. Here's a hint: it consists of just one word.* Write the students' ideas in two lists under the headings "music" and "title". After that, show students the short film. They will then meet Tommy Carroll and realize that he is blind. In my own experience, most students like the film.

From here, try to involve students in a discussion about the film. Ask questions that require them to look at it more critically. Here is a list of sample questions that you can ask as you conduct a discussion:

- *Do you think that the music is a good choice? Why or why not? What music would you have chosen?*
- *How does the music make you feel about Tommy?*
- *Should we feel sorry for Tommy?*
- *Do you think that Tommy wants us to feel sorry for him?*
- *If the filmmakers had chosen different music, do you think that the film would have been so popular? Why or why not?*
- *Do you think that "Brave" is a good title for the film? Why or why not? What title would you have chosen?*

- *How do you know that Tommy is brave? Isn't he just following his passion? Is it right to make this assumption?*
- *Of course, Tommy's blindness is an important part of his story. But is it possible that the film focuses too much on it?*
- *Do you know what a stereotype is? Can you give an example?*
- *Do you think that this film portrays Tommy as a stereotype in any way?*

As a follow-up, ask students to look for images and videos in the media that depict people with disabilities. Ask them to consider how they are portrayed or represented. Is the focus on the individual? Or is the individual reduced to and defined by his or her disability? If so, are there any familiar stereotypes present? These include people with disabilities as inspirational heroes, objects of pity, or dependent on others.

Story: "I Love Watermelon" ⚠️

[1] Hart is a young American YouTuber who makes comedy and music videos. According to the description on her YouTube channel, she comes "from the lesbian side of the LGBT community".[2]

Like many YouTubers, Hart interacts with her audience through a variety of social media channels.[3] And she often gets asked a question that annoys her.[4] In one of her most popular videos, she decides to address it. This is what she says:

"Hey guys! It's Hart . . . Today I would like to answer a question that I get asked regularly. I love women and you guys are like, 'I don't understand. If you love women so much, how come you don't dress like one? Why are you dressing like something you don't like?'"[5]

She continues:
"Number one — I don't dress like anyone but myself.
Number two — I love watermelon."[6]

⌁ Video: "Watermelon"

As well as dealing with comedy and music videos, Hart often deals with issues of identity and sexuality. On YouTube, she uses the name Hartbeat. One of her most popular videos is simply titled "Watermelon".

After telling us that she likes watermelon, Hart dances around her living room wearing a bikini made out of real watermelon and ends by saying: "Just because you love something, doesn't mean you have to dress like it."

Discussion

Start by showing students a picture of Hart. You could show them a screen capture from her "Watermelon" video in which she stands facing the camera.

From here, tell students the story "I Love Watermelon" and pause to ask the following questions:

1. *Have you ever seen this person before? Can you guess what she does for a living?* (She is a YouTuber.)

2. *What does* LGBT *stand for?* (It stands for lesbian, gay, bisexual, and transgender.)

3. *Do you follow any YouTubers? Do they interact with their audience? If so, how?* YouTubers may interact with their audience through a number of different platforms. These include Twitter, Snapchat, and comments on YouTube.

4. *What do you think is the annoying question that Hart often gets asked?* Students may focus on Hart's sexuality and appearance. But encourage them to go further than that. What are the typical questions that a famous YouTuber could get asked? Here are some suggestions from my own students:
   - *Where do you buy your clothes?*
   - *Why don't you like men?*
   - *Have you ever been with a man?*
   - *Why is your hair two different colours?*
   - *Why did you start making videos?*
   - *How many subscribers do you have?*
   - *What kind of video camera do you use to make your videos?*

5. *Hart responds to this question. Can you guess what she says next?*

6. *So she loves watermelon. Can you explain?* Students will often see the link: Hart loves watermelon but doesn't dress like one. After hearing students' ideas, show them the video.

As a follow-up activity, ask students to think of an annoying question that they often get asked. Alternatively, ask them to think of an annoying comment that other people often make about their own appearance, tastes, lifestyle, identity, etc.

▶ **Students as Filmmakers**

You could ask students to make a talking head video, in which they do three things:

1. Talk about an annoying question or comment that is often directed at them.
2. Say who asks the question or makes the comment, and when.
3. Address the question or comment.

Make sure that students realize that they do not have to dance around their living rooms in watermelon bikinis.

▶ **Tips for English Language Teachers**

In her video, Hart makes use of some interesting examples of spoken English. You could draw attention to and ask questions about the following:

- She uses *like* to report speech. This is used in some informal spoken language, particularly in North America. It was started by younger people and has moved into British English.
- She uses *how come* instead of *why*. This is found in informal spoken language in varieties of American and British English.
- She says: *"Why are you dressing like something you don't like?"* as opposed to the more standard *"Why do you dress like something you don't like?"*

5.3 Video Editing

Since the early days of moving pictures, filmmakers have developed a huge range of editing techniques and principles for telling their stories. As viewers, we experience and enjoy these techniques each time we watch an onscreen production. They may trick us, thrill us, or elicit an emotional response from us. They draw our attention to what the filmmakers consider is important, and away from what they consider is not.

Despite the established and widespread use of video editing, many of us are unaware of the techniques and principles that it involves. After all, it is difficult to follow a story and pay attention to technicalities at the same time. This is why film editing is sometimes called "the invisible art". But things are changing. As more and more of us become amateur videomakers, many of us are discovering editing techniques for ourselves.

The story in this section introduces students to a fundamental editing technique that is easy to take for granted.

Story: "The Kuleshov Effect"

Once upon a time, a singer wrote a song.

Over the years, the song became extremely popular. People all over the world loved it. It became "the beautiful song". And when the singer died, he became a legend.

One day another musician arrived in a town. The musician shouted at the townspeople: "I am the greatest living rock star on the planet!"

The townspeople gave him a stage and said: "Come on then! Show us."

The musician stepped onto the stage and started to sing. He sang the beautiful song. This seemed to please the townspeople. They sang along with him. They clapped and cheered.

But one man was not happy. His name was Samuel.

"This musician is not the greatest living rock star on the planet", said Samuel. "His performance of the beautiful song was terrible. His voice was flat. And he couldn't reach the high notes."

Samuel decided that he would teach the musician a lesson. Samuel was trained in a traditional craft known as video editing. Using his skills, he was able to resurrect the legendary singer. And he was able to show the world exactly what the legendary singer thought of the arrogant musician's performance.

The musician felt mocked. He was very angry. But there was nothing that he could do. He could not make people unsee what they had already seen.

And that is the end of the story. But to this day, Samuel's message can still be seen – a warning from history to other arrogant musicians. And those with access to the ancient internet can still see it on YouTube: the musician performing the beautiful song to the townspeople. Meanwhile, the legendary singer watches and laughs uncontrollably from the grave.

Video: "Kanye West Versus Freddie Mercury"

Glastonbury is a town in the southwest of England. It is home to the most famous music festival in the world. In 2015, hip hop artist Kanye West was selected to headline the festival. This proved to be a controversial decision. And despite a petition against his appearance, the performance went ahead.

One of the songs that Kanye West performed was "Bohemian Rhapsody" by the band Queen, whose lead singer was Freddie Mercury. And toward the end of the show, West told the crowd that they were watching "the greatest living rock star on the planet". Not surprisingly, his performance polarized critics.

One month after the festival, a videographer called Samuel Valorose created a mashup video, using footage of Kanye West's "Bohemian Rhapsody" Glastonbury performance with old footage of Freddie Mercury laughing. You can see the video on Samuel Valorose's website. You can access it at the accompanying website (see appendix 1 for information). Editing these together creates a cause-and-effect illusion in the mind of the viewer. To us, it seems as if Mercury is laughing at West for singing the song so badly. Of course, this couldn't possibly be the case – Freddie Mercury died in 1991. This video-editing phenomenon was first demonstrated by the Soviet film-maker Lev Kuleshov in the 1910s and 1920s. It is called the Kuleshov effect.

Incidentally, I spoke with Samuel Valorose about his video. Contrary to the story that I have written, Samuel is a big Kanye West fan and, like many of us, can't help but admire his arrogance. He created the video as a way of making fun of Kanye's bad performance of "Bohemian Rhapsody". Nothing more than that!

Discussion

For this activity to work, it is not important for students to know about Kanye West, Freddie Mercury, Queen, "Bohemian Rhapsody", or Glastonbury Festival. Here is a suggested way of using the story and video in the classroom:

1. Tell the story "The Kuleshov Effect", and as you tell the story, pause and invite students to ask you questions. Common questions may include the following:
   - *Is this a real story?*
   - *Who is the legendary singer?*
   - *Who is the arrogant musician?*
   - *Where is the town?*

   Tell students that the story might be true. Ask them to guess who the characters could be. Even if students don't know about Kanye West and Freddie Mercury, they may have some ideas based on their own pop cultures.

2. When you finish the story, tell students that it is based on real events. Allow students to ask more questions if they wish.

3. Tell students about Kanye West's appearance at Glastonbury in 2015 (described above). If necessary, let students hear the song "Bohemian Rhapsody" and make use of an image search site to show pictures of Kanye West and Freddie Mercury.

4. The important question to ask now is: *What do you expect Samuel's video to look like?* Make it clear that:
   - The video shows Kanye West performing "Bohemian Rhapsody" at Glastonbury in 2015.
   - It also shows Freddie Mercury laughing at West's performance.
   - Freddie Mercury died in 1991 so he couldn't possibly have been at Glastonbury in 2015.
   - The two singers never met.

5. At this stage, students may have some more questions for you. Answer these and address any confusion that they may have.

6. Tell students that you are going to let them see Samuel's video. But first, you want them to imagine how it appears. Ask students to create a simple storyboard – a series of quick sketches – to show what they think the video will look like. Give students a while to do this activity and then ask them to share their work with you and each other.

7. In my experience, students will usually assume that the video is more complex than it actually is. For example, students may want to retell the whole story from beginning to end. Others may think that visual effects are necessary. Bring this to your students' attention. Give them the following information:
   - *The video is probably more simple than you think.*
   - *No visual effects are involved, just editing.*
   - *Kanye West and Freddie Mercury do not appear in the same frame.*

- *You can probably capture the essence of the video in just two frames - in other words, a storyboard which consists of just two sketches.*

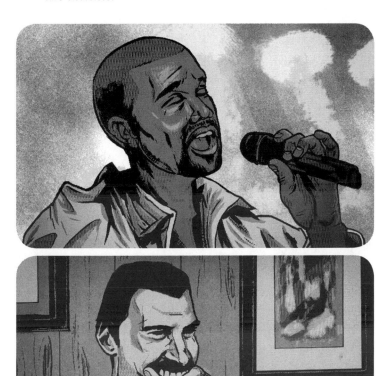

8. Ask students to make a second attempt at their storyboards. Then ask them to share their work with you and each other once again.

9. Show students the video. Draw their attention to the Kuleshov effect and ask students if they can think of any

other ways in which it could be used. Note that the story "Terrified" (chapter 2) is based on a short video which provides another great example of the effect.

As a follow-up task, you could ask students to find out about the story behind this technique. They could investigate the experiments that Lev Kuleshov carried out in the late 1910s and early 1920s. These demonstrated that if you take two shots and play them in sequence, the viewer will create a new meaning that is not present in either shot in isolation. In other words, the technique can be used to manipulate events to create new stories and interpretations. These experiments have been re-created many times, and many of the resulting videos can be found online, including one by Alfred Hitchcock.

► **Subject Connections**

For teachers of media and film studies, this activity could be used to introduce many other filmmaking and film-editing techniques. You could assign different techniques to different students and ask them to investigate them for homework. Here are a few possibilities:

- different types of transitions and cuts (dissolves, wipes, L cuts, jump cuts, smash cuts)
- split screen
- long takes
- use of B-roll (mentioned in chapter 1 regarding the story "Always Misunderstood")

Students could find examples of films, directors, and editors famous for using certain techniques, and describe the effects that they have on the viewer.

5.4 Visual Effects

Is it my imagination or has the internet seen an increase in UFOS caught on camera in the last few years? What's going on? Are we being invaded by aliens? Or is it possible that more and more amateur filmmakers are learning how to use visual effects software?

In this section, I would like to introduce Captain Disillusion, a YouTuber who understands the principles of visual effects and dedicates his time to exposing those who would like to fool us.

Story: "Captain Disillusion Versus the Tumba Ping Pong Show"

Part One: Miss Ping

The Tumba Ping Pong Show is a Swedish YouTube-based performing arts group. It consists of six men who dress in identical blue jackets and black jeans. They call themselves Little John, DJ Coolman, Mr. Sandman, Slightly Mad Max, Dr. Ders, and Jokko-Yxxi.

All of the group's videos involve hitting various objects with table tennis bats (or paddles, if you prefer). Group members demonstrate incredible skill as they hit ping pong balls into each other's mouths, eggs into frying pans, and darts into fruit.

So far, their most popular video is titled "Miss Ping". The video was filmed outdoors in a public area. Their special guest, Miss Ping, is dressed in pink. She stands confidently with a table tennis bat in each hand. Slightly Mad Max stands in front of her with two large kitchen knives – one in each hand. He puts one of the knives between his teeth and, with his free hand, he takes a table tennis bat out of his back pocket.

Slightly Mad Max holds up the first kitchen knife. With his table tennis bat, he hits the knife hard at Miss Ping. It spins through the air and sticks into the bat that Miss Ping is holding in her right

▶

hand. Slightly Mad Max takes the second knife from his mouth and does the same. This one sticks into the table tennis bat that Miss Ping is holding in her left hand.

At that moment, DJ Coolman appears in the frame. He stands behind Miss Ping with a pineapple. He holds it above Miss Ping's head. Slightly Mad Max takes a third kitchen knife from his back pocket. He hits the knife toward the pineapple and cuts it in half. The top part of the fruit falls to the ground.

Finally, Slightly Mad Max takes a ping pong ball out of his jacket pocket. He hits it as hard as he can at Miss Ping's face. Miss Ping catches the ping pong ball in her mouth.

Part Two: Captain Disillusion

YouTuber Captain Disillusion is a colourful character. He appears in his videos wearing a yellow jacket and black leather gloves, and the bottom half of his face painted silver. His catch phrase is "Love with your heart, use your head for everything else!"

Captain Disillusion is an expert in visual effects. He is a hero of rational thought and an exposer of YouTube hoaxes.

So far, Captain Disillusion has exposed dozens of viral videos as being fake. These include videos which feature ghosts, UFOs, mysterious floating cities and – now – knives and table tennis bats.

Six weeks after the "Miss Ping" video was uploaded onto YouTube, the Tumba Ping Pong Show became the subject of one of Captain Disillusion's videos.

Captain Disillusion showed that the "Miss Ping" video was fake. He drew attention to a range of techniques that the Tumba Ping Pong Show used to fool viewers into thinking that the knife throwing, pineapple cutting, and ping pong ball catching were real. The Tumba Ping Pong Show had its first enemy.

Part Three: Miss Pong

A few weeks later, the Tumba Ping Pong Show uploaded a new video. This one was called "Miss Pong". The format was the same as the "Miss Ping" video but some details were different.

Instead of kitchen knives, Slightly Mad Max hits circular saw blades at Miss Pong's table tennis bats. And instead of a pineapple, DJ Coolman holds a coconut above Miss Pong's head.

At the end of the video, a stranger in a yellow jacket walks into the background of the frame. When he sees Miss Pong, DJ Coolman, and Slightly Mad Max, he stops."Who are these people and what are they doing?" Then he sees the circular saw blades. He decides that it might be safer to walk away. But before he can do that, Slightly Mad Max takes a hammer out of his back pocket. He hits it hard with his table tennis bat. It spins over Miss Pong's head and hits the stranger directly on the forehead. He cries out in pain and falls to the floor, holding his head in agony.

Was that an accident? Or did Slightly Mad Max do it on purpose? Maybe this was an act of revenge.

Videos: "Miss Ping", "Miss Ping Debunk", and "Miss Pong"

The three videos referred to in this story can all be seen on YouTube. As always, you can find links to them on the accompanying website (see appendix 1). The videos are titled as follows: "Miss Ping" (Tumba Ping Pong Show), "Miss Ping Debunk" (Captain Disillusion), and "Miss Pong" (Tumba Ping Pong Show).

Discussion

"Captain Disillusion Versus the Tumba Ping Pong Show" is quite a long story. And for many students, it will be difficult to follow if you read it aloud to them. Despite this, there is a lot that we can do with the story and the videos that it is based on. Rather than offer a step-by-step procedure for using these videos in the classroom, I would like to offer some ideas and suggestions.

1. Give out copies of the text: You can make scans, screen captures, or photocopies of the story and distribute them to your students for them to read themselves. You might want to plan things so that you give out different parts of the story at different times.

2. Omit Part One of the story: Part One is quite complex. You could choose to go straight to the Tumba Ping Pong Show's YouTube channel and introduce the group to your students by showing a few of their videos, including the video "Miss Ping".

3. Use isolated story items: Tell students that they are going to see a video in which three people perform a very dangerous stunt. Tell them that it involves the following: three table tennis bats (or paddles, if you prefer), three large kitchen knives, a pineapple, and a ping pong ball. Ask students to predict what happens in the video. In order to do this, they can ask you questions.

4. Have students act out the "Miss Ping" stunt: Not with real knives! Put students into groups of three: Student 1 is Miss Ping; Student 2 is Slightly Mad Max; Student 3 is DJ Coolman. Tell the students to imagine that they are going to perform a very dangerous stunt involving the objects listed in the idea above. Talk them through the idea so that they mime the action (but do not actually throw objects and hurt themselves):

Okay, let's start with Miss Ping. Miss Ping - you are holding two table tennis bats - one in each hand. Slightly Mad Max - I want you to stand in front of Miss Ping so that you are facing each other but leave some space between you. Slightly Mad Max - you are holding two large kitchen knives, one in each hand. There is also a table tennis bat in your back pocket. Now put one of the kitchen knives between your teeth, and with your free hand, take the table tennis bat out of your back pocket. Now when I count to three, Slightly Mad Max, you are going to hit the knife hard at Miss Ping. And Miss Ping, you are going to block the knife with one of your table tennis bats. The knife is going to stick into it. Are you ready? One, two, three - go!

Slightly Mad Max - take the second knife from out of your mouth and do the same. Miss Ping - you will block this knife with your other table tennis bat. Are you ready? One, two, three - go!

Now, DJ Coolman - you are holding a pineapple. I want you to stand behind Miss Ping and hold the pineapple just above her head. Keep your fingers out of the way. Slightly Mad Max - you will find another knife in your other back pocket. Take it out. Now hit it with your table tennis bat and try to cut the pineapple in half. Are you ready? One, two, three - go!

And finally - Slightly Mad Max - there is a ping pong ball in your jacket pocket. Take it out. You are going to hit it at Miss Ping's face as hard as you can. Miss Ping - you are going to catch the table ping pong ball in your mouth. Are you ready? One, two, three - go!

After getting students to try out this stunt, ask them if they think that it would really be possible to perform it. Ask students how long it would take to plan and ask them to consider the dangers that might be involved. Then introduce students to the Tumba Ping Pong Show and let them see the "Miss Ping" video.

5. Let students wonder whether the events are real: When you show students the Tumba Ping Pong Show's videos, do not tell them that visual effects have been used to create them. If you are lucky, some clever or skeptical individual in the classroom will raise this question. If not, tell your students that some people have posted comments on YouTube to say that the video is not real. Then take a vote. Find out who

thinks the video is real and who thinks that it is not. Ask students to give reasons for their answers. You will have to play the video a few more times during this process.

6. Use images to enhance your story: Online, there are many images of Captain Disillusion and the Tumba Ping Pong Show. Create a slideshow of images to show students as you tell your story and introduce the characters.

7. Ask students how the "Miss Ping" video was created: Tell students that you know for a fact that the video is not real. Put students into groups and ask them to speculate how it was created. You will have to play the video a number of times so that students can watch carefully and share their ideas.

8. Introduce students to Captain Disillusion: Read Part Two of the story to your students and tell them about Captain Disillusion. Then play his "Miss Ping Debunk" video. Ask students to watch, listen carefully, and make notes. They should try to list all of the techniques described by Captain Disillusion that were used to create the "Miss Ping" video. This could be done as homework. English language learners in particular might appreciate this; they could watch the video as many times as they like and pay attention to some of the terminology that Captain Disillusion uses.

9. Ask students to predict: Tell students that the story isn't finished yet and ask them to guess what happens next. Remind them that the Tumba Ping Pong Show now had their first enemy (as mentioned at the end of Part Two in the story). Ask students to guess how the Tumba Ping Pong Show got their revenge on Captain Disillusion. Read Part Three of the story and ask students if they can explain the last line: *Was that an accident? Or did he do it on purpose? Maybe this was an act of revenge?* Finally, show students the third video: "Miss Pong". At the end of the video, they will see a man who looks like Captain Disillusion getting hit on the head by a hammer.

▶ **Visual Effects and Online Video**

There are many visual effects software possibilities for non-professionals. But, make no mistake – it takes a lot of time and effort to learn to use them. Applying visual effects involves working with individual frames in the video. This can be a laborious process. For example, according to Captain Disillusion, the creators of the "Miss Ping" video had to hide some things that they didn't want us to see (e.g. painting over the tips of the knives in the table tennis bats) and add some new things that were never there in the first place (e.g. the individual images of the spinning knives or flying ping pong ball).

▶ **Students as Videotellers**

The Captain Disillusion character was created by Alan Melikdjanian, a visual effects expert who lives in the United States. His YouTube channel has a lot of excellent videos that expose many viral videos as being fake. Although Alan Melikdjanian's specialty is visual effects, he often goes beyond that to explore what motivates people to create fake videos. He also refers to cases of uncritical news reporting and lazy journalism – sensational stories that originated from fake videos that should never have made it into the mainstream media.

Ask students to choose a Captain Disillusion video that they like and do the following:

- Describe the video that Captain Disillusion refers to.
- Tell the story behind the video that Captain Disillusion examines: *When was it created? How many views did it get? Was it reported by mainstream media?*
- Summarize how Captain Disillusion exposes it as being fake.

▶ **Subject Connections**
This story will be of particular interest to teachers of film and media studies. Students could investigate the history and development of special and visual effects in filmmaking. French magician and filmmaker Georges Méliès would be a good place to start.

5.5 Honesty

Over the years, the traditional mass media (mainly newspapers, TV, and radio) in many countries has developed codes of practice - ethics and standards for journalists, broadcasters, and documentary makers - as well as expectations from consumers. Of course, it would be naive to assume that these codes are always upheld. But they do exist.

Unfortunately, the same cannot be said for the newer social media. Virtually anyone can publish blog posts, podcasts, or videos without any form of quality control and without the need to answer to an audience. And at a time when it is becoming increasingly difficult for voices to get heard online, some people are resorting to questionable practices to gain attention.

Story: "Honesty Test"
An actor who pretends to be a blind man walks around the streets of Adelaide in Australia. He approaches various people and asks for change for a $5 bill. But in his hand he holds a $50 bill.
Will anyone take advantage of this situation?

Apparently, yes. Out of the ten people that he approaches, four men and one woman choose to give the man change for $5 and take his $50 bill.

▶

The actor who plays the blind man is a well-known Australian YouTuber called Adrian Gee. When he released this "social experiment" video in November 2015, it immediately went viral and received a lot of attention from national and international media. Adrian Gee started to make TV appearances.

After watching the social experiment video, a chat show host holds his head in disbelief and asks: "What is wrong with this world?"

"What drove you to try this out?" asks an interviewer.

"I wanted to do something based on honesty", replies Adrian.

So are the people of Adelaide particularly dishonest people? Or does the social experiment reflect the true nature of human beings in general? Perhaps motivated to find out the answer, a local current affairs programme called *Today Tonight* decided to investigate the individuals in the video. And when they did, they made an interesting discovery.

Videos: "The Real Blind Man Honesty Test (Social Experiment)" and "Honesty Hoax"

This story is based on two videos. The first is titled "The Real Blind Man Honesty Test (Social Experiment)". You can see it on Adrian Gee's YouTube channel. The second video is a news report by Australian current affairs programme *Today Tonight*. You can see the video on their website. As always, you can access this on the accompanying website (see appendix 1 for information).

Whereas other media channels reported the story of Adrian Gee's honesty test without question, *Today Tonight* revealed that everyone who appeared in the so-called "social experiment" video was an actor. They were all following Adrian Gee's directions. In other words, the video was completely staged. And to make it worse, some of the actors had no idea that they would be portrayed as real-life thieves.

Discussion

In the film "Blind Luck" [page 94], a dishonest shopkeeper unsuccessfully tries to keep a blind man's winning lottery ticket. The activity described below would be a good follow-up.

1. If they haven't already seen it, show your students the film "Blind Luck".

2. Ask students if they are familiar with the term "social experiment". Find out if anyone has seen any social experiments on YouTube and if so, ask them to describe them. Note that social experiments are often associated with psychology. For example, they can allow researchers to investigate how people behave in certain situations. However, the term seems to have become a bit of an overused buzzword on sites like YouTube. At worst, there is a thin line between so-called "social experiment" videos and "prank videos" (i.e. practical jokes caught on camera).

3. Give students the following task: *Imagine that you want to design a social experiment to see if people would take advantage of a blind man in the way that Matthew tried to take advantage of David. How would you do it? It doesn't have to take place in a shop and it doesn't have to involve a scratch card.*

4. Ask students to share their ideas with you and each other.

5. Tell students that they are going to see a social experiment video which deals with honesty. Tell students that the social experiment involves the following items:
    - *a $5 bill*
    - *a $50 bill*
    - *an actor pretending to be a blind man*

- *several members of the public*
- *several hidden cameras*
- *the streets of Adelaide* (a city in South Australia)

6. Ask students to predict the nature of the social experiment. How exactly does it work?

7. Refer to the story "Honesty Test" and tell students how the social experiment works. Tell students that the actor playing the blind man approaches six men and four women. Ask students to predict how many men and how many women are dishonest. In other words, how many of them take the $50 bill and give back change from $5?

	MEN (6)	WOMEN (4)
HONEST		
DISHONEST		

8. Show students the first video "The Real Blind Man Honesty Test (Social Experiment)". They will see that out of the ten people, four men and one woman are dishonest. Find out which of your students came closest to predicting these results.

9. Ask students the following questions:
   - *How do you feel about these results?*
   - *Do they surprise you at all? In what way?*
   - *How do you feel about the people in the video?*

10. If students feel disgusted by the dishonest people in the video, ask them which person in the video they dislike the most and why. Play the video a second time, if necessary, and ask students to share their thoughts.

11. If at this stage no one has questioned the authenticity of the social experiment video, tell students that they have all failed the test! Ask them to guess why this could be.

12. Tell students that a current affairs programme called *Today Tonight* decided to investigate the social experiment and the people in it. Tell students that they made an interesting discovery. Ask students to guess what the current affairs programme found out.

13. Play the first six minutes of the second video "Honesty Hoax". Stop it just before the reporter confronts Adrian Gee and accuses him of being a fake. Ask students to discuss the following questions:
    - *Now which person in the video disgusts you the most?*
    - *Why do you think someone would choose to stage a video like this? In other words, why would they use actors instead of real people?*
    - *If the "social experiment" is a lie, then what was the point in creating it? Why would someone like Adrian Gee be dishonest?*

14. Play the rest of the video. Some of these questions are answered. Ask students if there is anything that they can learn from this story.

Why Lie?

Anyone who works in video production knows that when filming in public places, everything that can go wrong does go wrong. It is much easier to stage an event than capture it naturally on camera. So, in order to get the job done efficiently, actors are always an option in cases like this. As well as practical reasons, there are also legal reasons for using actors. If you want to be on the right side of the law, you must get individuals who appear in your videos to sign a release form. Members of the public will often refuse to do that.

Viral videos are valuable commodities. As reported by *Today Tonight*, Adrian Gee will have earned money from his so-called "social experiment". And of course, there are always people who will prioritize money and media attention over integrity and respectability.

We should also remember that most prominent YouTubers are young people. Adrian Gee was twenty-two years old when he created his fake social experiment video. And although that is no excuse, youth is the time in life for making mistakes. I don't know about you, but at the age of twenty-two, I wasn't the responsible individual that I am today.

So, what can we learn from this story? Well, perhaps we should question the authenticity of everything that we see on screen - whether we are considering amateur online videos or professional mainstream news broadcasters. That may sound obvious. But I have used this activity with a lot of people - both students and teachers - and only very occasionally does someone question the authenticity of the "social experiment" video.

But how skeptical should we be? In the words of Captain Disillusion (see previous activity): "The power to tell real from fake doesn't come from being a world expert or mistrusting every single thing you see. It comes from an honest willingness to change your opinions and beliefs based on new facts. So learn to enjoy being wrong. The world might start making more sense."

► **Subject Connections**

This activity will be of particular interest to teachers of ethics and media studies. Ask students to consider who was less responsible: Adrian Gee for creating a bogus social experiment or the mainstream media outlets that reported his story without investigating it.

Teachers of media studies, ethics, and sociology will also be interested in the following case study.

► **A Critical Case Study**

One of the best-known viral videos from 2014 is titled "10 Hours of Walking in New York City as a Woman". It was created by filming a twenty-four-year-old woman with a hidden camera as she silently walked around the streets of Manhattan. The two-minute video consists of a montage of verbal harassment from men. It was featured in the mainstream media and has its own entry page on Wikipedia.

As well as getting a lot of people talking, the viral video drew a lot of criticism. Among other things, the feminist group that commissioned the video and the advertising agency that produced it were accused of several failings.

- A faulty definition of harassment: The video failed to differentiate between serious harassment and friendly or well-intended street interactions.
- Discrimination: Many of the men in the video were African Americans. Virtually all of the men came from lower socio-economic backgrounds.
- Dishonesty: The advertising agency used a number of techniques to manipulate their story. Whereas some saw the video as proof of an epidemic problem, Christina Hoff Sommers from *The Factual Feminist* blog called it propaganda. On the accompanying website, you can access Christina Hoff Sommers's video critique of "10 Hours of Walking in New York City as a Woman" (see appendix 1 for information).

This story provides a fascinating case study. It opens up many complex issues that teachers of ethics, sociology, and media studies might want to address. Show the video to your students and ask them what they think of it. Then ask them to explore, discuss, and give their own opinions about the various reasons for which it was criticized.

5.6 Exploring the Internal Narrative

They say that every picture tells a story. But as we have seen throughout this book, this is not exactly true. Any picture can be associated with an infinite number of stories. And importantly, it is us, the viewers, that construct or "tell" them - not the picture.

In this last section, we will look at two activities that aim to raise students' awareness of the diversity of interpretations. The activities are slightly different to the others in the book. The first activity focuses on a well-known photograph of an event that was also captured on video. The second activity starts with a video and then moves onto the story - a reversal of the Videotelling norm.

The following story is a description of a photograph – not a video. It is an exploration of my own internal narrative. As you read it, consider how your own interpretation is different from mine.

Story: "Love and Chaos"

For me, this is a romantic image. It seems to communicate a contrast between love on one hand and chaos on the other. In the centre of the picture, a young man and a young woman are kissing passionately. They are surrounded by protesters and riot police. The man and woman don't seem to care what is happening around them. I imagine that they met for the first time that day. They were strangers in the crowd. Their eyes met and, overcome with mutual attraction, they moved toward each other and embraced. In doing so, they are launching their own spontaneous demonstration within a demonstration. By kissing, they want to show the world that love is the way.

They are referencing the famous slogan: "Make love, not war".

Image and Video: "Vancouver Riot Kissing Couple"

The story refers to an iconic photograph from 2011. Photojournalist Richard Lam took the picture during the Stanley Cup riots in Vancouver. (The Stanley Cup is a hockey tournament held annually.) It is easy to find the photograph and read about the story online (see appendix 1).

After the photograph dominated the western world's media for a number of days, an amateur video emerged. The video showed what happened before and after the moment at which the photograph was taken. Although the video quality is bad, you can identify the woman from her green top. The video shows the couple being knocked to the ground by some charging riot police. We then hear the woman sobbing – possibly in pain - and the man comforting her. The footage can be seen on the accompanying website (see appendix 1).

Discussion

The story "Love and Chaos" refers to my own internal narrative. It is the story that I imagined without knowing anything else about the photograph. In other words, it is purely interpretive and speculative.

For this activity, I suggest that you create a similar story based on your own internal narrative. However, you are more than welcome to use mine and pretend that it is your own. I promise that I won't tell your students! Here is an activity based on my own internal narrative - the "Love and Chaos" story.

1. Tell students that you are going to describe an image to them. Tell them to listen carefully and decide whether or not they have seen the image before.

2. Read the story "Love and Chaos" to your students. You can read it directly from this book. Do not let students see the image.

3. Find out if anyone thinks that they can identify the image. If so, ask them to describe it in more detail.

4. Show students the photograph. If you have a projector, you can find the image online and display it on a big screen in the class. Importantly, if anyone knows the story behind the image, ask them to forget everything that they know about it. In other words, ask them to pretend that they have never seen it before.

5. Tell students that your description of the photograph is not based on fact. It is your own personal interpretation - the story that you created in your imagination in response to it.

Tell students that you are going to describe it again and this time you want them to decide whether or not they agree with you.

6. Read the story a second time. This time, students should be able to see the image on the screen. As you tell the story, pause and ask students whether or not they agree with the following:
   - *It is a romantic image.*
   - *It communicates a contrast between love on one hand and chaos on the other.*
   - *Passion is the motive behind the kiss.*
   - *The man and woman don't care what is happening around them.*
   - *They met for the first time that day.*
   - *They are launching their own spontaneous demonstration within a demonstration.*
   - *They want to show the world that love is the way. They are referencing the famous slogan: "Make love, not war".*

   In each case, ask for a show of hands: Who agrees with you and who does not? Invite students to give their opposing opinions and justify their answers. Try to hear as many different ideas as possible. Some students may question whether or not the man and woman are actually kissing.

7. Point out to students that although there is only one photograph, everyone creates a different story in response to it. Tell students that they are going to put their own imagined stories into words. Ask them to write a paragraph in which they speculate about the people in the picture and the incident. You could give a word limit (one hundred words, for example).

8. Once students have done this, put them into groups and ask them to share their stories with each other. Later, you can put the stories on the classroom wall or class blog so that they can be seen by everyone.

9. Tell students that when the photographer took the photograph, someone was filming the scene on the street from a balcony. Tell them that you are going to show them the video. Before you do this, ask students to predict what happened before and what happened after the moment captured in the photograph.

10. Play the video. You will probably have to do this a couple of times and let students identify the woman from her green top.

11. Ask students to return to the stories that they created. Ask them to consider how their ideas have changed now that they have seen the video. People who originally thought that the photograph was romantic may change their mind at this point. And many people will question whether or not there was actually a kiss.

12. Finally, ask students to discuss what they can learn from all this. Elicit ideas and aim for a class discussion. Here are some points that could be raised:
    - The media often romanticizes reality.
    - However, the media caters to what the public desires. It provides us with the stories that we want to read, hear, and see. This photograph seems to contain certain ingredients that make it particularly appealing to mass tastes.
    - A picture does not tell a story. Any picture can be associated with an infinite number of stories that we create in our own minds.
    - The stories that we create in response to an image can change at any time. This can depend on how much we see in the image as well as the facts that we find out about it. We may also be influenced by other people's interpretations. For example, if the media tells us that the couple is kissing, then we might agree without question.

As a follow-up task, ask students to go online and investigate the story behind the riot kiss photograph. Students could find out about the story behind the riot, the kissing couple, or the photographer, Richard Lam. There are some good resources online that you can direct them to, if necessary. Some of these are accessible on the accompanying website (see appendix 1).

▶ **Tips for English Language Teachers**

My story "Love and Chaos" contains a number of words and phrases that demonstrate that the ideas are personal interpretations:

- *It seems to . . .*
- *I would say that . . .*
- *I imagine that . . .*
- *I think that . . .*
- *Perhaps . . .*

Refer your students to these before they write their own texts.

▶ **Subject Connections**

This activity will be of interest to teachers of art, media studies, law, and citizenship. It can be used to introduce the subjects of photo-journalism, citizen journalism, rioting, and law and order.

Story: The Story Behind "Sneezing Baby Panda"

"She levitated in shock and looked at us – if you follow her eyes, you can see that's what she's doing. And we levitated in shock and looked back at her because we'd been there for ages and nothing had happened. And we said to the cameraman: *You have got the camera rolling, haven't you?* And he said yes."

In 1999, Australian wildlife documentary producers Lesley Hammond and Jenny Walsh were in Sichuan province in China.

▶

They were filming a documentary about giant pandas at the Wolong Panda Center. According to Lesley: "We normally film pandas in their own habitats. But this was a documentary about panda breeding and in the wild; you could never get that on camera."

One of their subjects was Mao Mao, an adult female who had recently given birth. The team was hoping to capture some interaction between her and her six-week-old cub, Chi Chi. Malcolm the cameraman had already set up his equipment beside the enclosure. But on that day, nothing interesting was happening.

Mao Mao seemed more interested in her nutritional cookies than her cub. According to Lesley: "She put her baby on the ground and she was feeding her face with this biscuit, and absolutely going for it. And out of nowhere, her baby made that noise. The truth is it's not sneezing – it's screaming for attention. It's like any human baby – the mother is completely ignoring it and the baby wants attention. And that's what's really happening in that clip."

"So what happened next?" I asked Lesley during our Skype call.

"Well, having looked at us, Mao Mao kept eating with one hand. And with her other hand, she leant down to pick up her baby and comfort him. But she never stopped eating."

ᗡ Video: "Sneezing Baby Panda"

This activity makes use of the "Sneezing Baby Panda" video which, at the time of writing, is the most popular animal video on YouTube. According to YouTube folklore, the panda cub let out a powerful, high-pitched sneeze. But according to producer Lesley Hammond, it was a cry for attention. "The Story Behind Sneezing Baby Panda" is based on a Skype interview that I had with Lesley Hammond in 2014. I filmed the call and you can see the video on my YouTube channel (see the accompanying website).

In 2015, Lesley Hammond and Jenny Walsh released *Sneezing Baby Panda: The Movie*. It tells the fictitious story of an Australian zoologist who goes in search of the sneezing baby panda in a quest to save her struggling zoo.

Discussion

This activity can serve as an experiment in perception and interpretation. The activity has a basic four-part structure:

1. Students watch the video "Sneezing Baby Panda" and then write a description of it.

2. Students compare their descriptions and in doing so, compare their interpretations of the video and in particular, the assumptions that they make about it.

3. Students ask questions about the video.

4. You tell students "The Story Behind Sneezing Baby Panda".

It is very likely that some students will have seen the video before. Those students may be aware that the video is titled "Sneezing Baby Panda". For this experiment to work, that information should not be passed to the students who have not seen the video. For this reason, the first part of the activity should be done in silence.

Similarly, when you play the video in class, set things up so that students do not see the video title on the screen. In order to make this possible, Lesley and Jenny have given me permission to upload the video on my own YouTube channel with the title "What's Going On Here?" (see appendix 1).

Here is one way to set up the experiment:

1. Give students the following instruction: *Today, we are going to do an experiment. I am going to show you a short YouTube*

video. It is possible that you have seen it before. When you watch it, I want you to be absolutely silent. And once you have seen it, no talking! Are you ready?

2. Play the video "Sneezing Baby Panda". If anyone laughs, tell them off. Remind students that they should not say a word at this stage.

3. Tell students: *Now what I want you to do is write a short description of what you have just seen. I want you to describe the video from beginning to end. You can aim for around fifty words. Before you do that, would you like to see it again?*

4. Play the video a second and third time, and continue to tell off students if they laugh.

5. Ask students to write their descriptions of the video. They should do this without helping each other. If you are an English language teacher, you can give students access to bilingual dictionaries to translate from their own language into English.

6. Once everyone has done this, invite students to read out their descriptions to the rest of the class.

7. Ask students to consider what assumptions they made about the video and the pandas. Ask students to put up their hands if they made any of the following conclusions:
   - *the big panda is female*
   - *the little panda is the big panda's baby*
   - *the video was filmed in a zoo*
   - *the big panda is eating bamboo*
   - *the little panda is sleeping*
   - *the little panda sneezes*

8. Ask students if there are any other assumptions that they made, details that they described or questions that they considered.

9. Find out who has already seen the video and who has not. For those who have seen it, find out what they know about it. There is usually very little to say here except that it is a viral video on YouTube that has come to be known as "Sneezing Baby Panda".

Ask students to consider where the video might have come from, who might have created it, and why. One common suggestion is that the panda incident was caught on camera by a visitor to a zoo. The problem with this, however, is that it looks too professional – the camera is obviously mounted on a tripod and the frame is well composed. Another common suggestion is that it has come from closed-circuit television (CCTV). But you would expect a CCTV camera to be mounted at a higher position and to have a complete view of the panda's enclosure. In addition, CCTV footage is usually in black and white, and without audio.

10. Tell students that you are going to tell them the story behind the panda video. Read them "The Story Behind Sneezing Baby Panda". You can also show them my Skype interview with Lesley Hammond (see appendix 1 for information on how to access it).

Interpreting the Experiment

In my experience, most people who are already familiar with the video and its title will describe the baby panda's action as a sneeze. However, people not familiar with the video may offer more diverse interpretations (hiccups, yelps, screams, shrieks, screeches, etc.). Find out if this applies to your students and ask them what we can learn from this experiment. Here are some ideas:

• Internal narratives: Although there is only one "Sneezing Baby Panda" video, different people will interact with it and interpret it in different ways. Importantly, our internal narratives are always subject to change depending on what we see, how we are influenced, and what we find out.

- Assumed "facts" and misrepresentations: The title of the video tells us that the baby panda sneezes. And collectively, many of us will accept this without question. I would be surprised if Chi Chi the panda cub was unhappy about this misrepresentation. But in other cases, assumptions can be harmful. Ask your students if they can think of any examples of harmful assumptions.

- External narratives: Every online video is an artifact. There is always a bigger picture to be explored. We can investigate any video by asking *who, what, when, where, why,* and *how* questions about it. Examples of specific questions were provided in chapter 1 [page 33].

Appendices

Appendix 1: Videos, Materials, and Resources

HROUGHOUT THIS BOOK, I have referred to many online videos, materials, and resources. You will find links to all of these on the accompanying website:

www.videotelling.com

At the beginning of each chapter, I have also included a QR code that will take you directly to the relevant links page (QR = "quick response"). This one will take you to the accompanying website.

In order to "read" a QR code, you will need the following:

- a mobile device (a smartphone or tablet computer)
- internet connection
- a QR code reader app (see below)

There are literally hundreds of QR code reader apps to choose from and many of them are free. In order to download one, visit the App Store (iPhones and iPads) or the Google Play

Store (Android devices) and search for QR *reader*. I have suggested a few of these on the accompanying website.

When you open the app, you can then "read" the QR code with the camera on your mobile device and the website will pop open. If you have never done this before, try it now.

On the accompanying website, I have also included some suggestions for apps and websites that allow you to create your own QR codes.

Appendix 2: Troubleshooting

I have used Videotelling activities in many different teaching and teacher-training contexts. I am very aware of the problems that can arise, as well as the questions and concerns that teachers can have. Here, I would like to address some of them.

I am not confident enough to tell a story in class.

A lot of teachers tell me this. Sometimes, I respond by asking: *"Does that mean that you never share personal anecdotes with your students?"* Their response is often: *"Well, yes. But that's different."*

There are as many ways to tell a story as there are human beings on the planet. Although we may think of storytellers as being performers - outgoing, confident, charismatic types - the stories in this book are created for the classroom, not the stage.

If you are new to storytelling, here are some tips:

- Practise, prepare, and reflect: An experienced storyteller can make it look easy and spontaneous. But success requires planning and reflection.
- Choose the right moment: Look for a time when everyone is in a good mood - Friday afternoon, just before the weekend, for example.

- Start small: Choose an activity in the book that is short and simple. The simpler the activity, the less there is to go wrong.
- Have a backup plan: For example, have photocopies of the story that you are using. If things don't go according to plan, give out copies of the story and turn the activity into one that involves reading.

Students have already seen the video.

Some of the videos in this book date to the early days of online video - as far back as 2006. A lot of people won't remember them, if indeed, they ever saw them in the first place. And even if students have seen a video, that doesn't mean that they will recall it when you tell the story.

In some cases, however, we will want to take precautions. For example, for the story "Splat!" (in chapter 4), after you have told students about the exploding watermelon, you could ask: *I wonder if anyone knows this. Don't say anything but put up your hand if you think you know how Gavin and Daniel caused the watermelon to explode.*

If any students put up their hands, ask them to whisper their ideas in your ear or write their answers and show them to you secretly. If you can identify any students who have seen the video, form a bond with them. Give them a wink, a nudge, or a high five. Make them believe that they have an advantage over the rest of the class and encourage them not to share their knowledge about the video with anyone else. For example, say: *It's really clever, isn't it? Do you think that anyone will guess how Gavin and Daniel caused the watermelon to explode?*

A student correctly guesses the element of surprise and spoils the story.

Here is a typical situation that I have witnessed many times in the Videotelling workshops that I give:

Teacher: *So yes, the mother is sitting in the corner, eating a snack.*
Participant: *Are they human? Is this the "Sneezing Baby Panda" video?*
Teacher: *Oh! Yes. How did you know?*

And that's it. The participant guesses the "answer" and the teacher stops there. No! Although a student may think that they know the video that you are describing, they can never be sure unless you tell them, there and then. So, how about the following instead:

Teacher: *So yes, the mother is sitting in the corner, eating a snack.*
Participant: *Are they human? Is this the "Sneezing Baby Panda" video?*
Teacher: *The "Sneezing Baby Panda" video? I think that I have seen that. Can you remind us what happens?... Oh yes, I remember it. So you think that the mother and the baby in this video are pandas?... That's interesting. We'll see...*

The surprise is only spoiled if you tell the class that the student guessed correctly. The clever student might suspect but cannot be sure. And the rest of the class will probably have no idea. Don't give in too easily. Entertain ideas and then continue. Moments like the one described will quickly be forgotten as you progress with the story.

Perhaps more importantly, we shouldn't be too precious about the element of surprise. In many cases, it is just one small part of the activity.

My students are impatient.
They say: "Why can't you just show us the video?"

For me, this is quite a familiar situation. Often, the solution is simple: Don't tell students that the story is based on a video. This will work in some cases but not in others.

You might also try a little white lie. Tell your students that the video is no longer online: *I'm really sorry. I was going to show you a video. But it's been removed from YouTube. So what I'm going to do is tell you about it.*

If students give you a really hard time, refer them to the 2011 film, *Detachment*, and the words of the teacher Henry Barthes, played by Adrien Brody: "How are you to imagine anything if the images are always provided for you?"

My students are disorderly.

Many of us might believe that the ideal group of students would be respectful and disciplined. They would listen intently and only speak when spoken to. But is this really what we would want? It sounds a bit dull to me.

The activities in this book are fun. They aim to get students thinking and speaking. And when young students and excitable tweens and teens (and sometimes even adults) have something to say, they don't always wait in line to say it.

In my experience, teacher-led storytelling will usually involve a certain amount of chaos. Try changing your expectations (not for quiet and restrained, but for engaged and possibly loud students) and work with this to the best of your abilities. You may get tired of constantly telling students not to shout out answers or not to speak when others are speaking. But in fact, it may be the only way. Of course, this will depend on the level of discipline that you command. But I should say that mine is not particularly high!

Sometimes, teacher enthusiasm can be a great motivator. If you can make students believe that they are going to enjoy the story, students may police themselves with this: *"Shhhhhh! Be quiet! We want to listen to this!"* It's always nice for a teacher to hear that.

In cases when you are really fighting to keep students' attention, try reducing the number of questions that you ask. Keep the story shorter and less interactive.

I have silent students who don't want to join in.

The consumption of narratives is not a passive process. Constructing an internal narrative requires imagination, visualization, prediction, and more. Sometimes, we feel the need to put this mental activity into words. But sometimes we do not. Do not assume that a silent student is a disengaged student. As storytellers in the classroom, it is our job to be as inclusive as possible and invite everyone to express their thoughts. But perhaps we shouldn't worry too much if some students decline the offer.

Mobile phones are banned in my school.

This might seem like a problem if you are interested in getting students to create video content of their own. But in fact, the classroom is not an ideal place for shooting videos. When many students are doing this at the same time, the result is noise pollution.

Fortunately, mobile devices open the learning space. If we want students to create videos of their own (discussed in appendix 4), this will generally work better outside the classroom - in the comfort of their homes, for example. Students can choose quiet locations which are more interesting or personal than the classroom. Video editing and video sharing can also be done outside the classroom. In this way, banned mobile phones should not be a problem.

I have no option to play the video in class.

The traditional way to use video in the classroom is to watch it first and talk about it later. The activities in this book reverse that process: questions, discussion, and analysis come first. Viewing comes second. This means that in many cases, you can do the story and activity in the classroom, and students can watch the video at home.

In such cases, provide students with instructions on how to find the video. Alternatively, put a link to the video on a class blog or similar online space. If mobile phones are not banned, one of my favourite approaches is to show students a QR code at the end of the story (see example below), ask them to take a photograph of it with their mobile device and use it to access the video later. There are many free QR code creator apps online (see the accompanying website).

Appendix 3: Storytelling Techniques

There are many techniques that you can use as you tell stories in the classroom. These serve to maximize student comprehension and engagement.

General Techniques

Read a Text Aloud

Reading aloud is an essential skill for any teacher. It requires not being a slave to the text in hand and communicating with "eyes up" as much as possible. Most importantly, reading aloud involves preparation. Familiarize yourself with the text and read it out a few times before taking it into class. Identify moments that require vocal punctuation (rising or falling intonation, attention to rhythm, phrasing, pause, etc.). Also familiarize yourself with the structure of the text - paragraphing, for example. This will allow you to quickly find your place when you move your eyes back to the paper.

Create Story Pathways

As an alternative to reading from notes, you can create a list of items and phrases that appear in the text in chronological order. I call this a "story pathway". Its function is to guide you through the basic structure and events of the story, and remind you of the specific ideas and phrases that you want to include. For example, when I tell the story *"Lepus arcticus"* (chapter 1), I use the following story pathway:

- *snowboarding down a mountain*
- *deep and untouched*
- *avalanche*
- *unaware of the danger*
- *continued down the slope*
- *from side to side*
- *getting stronger and stronger*
- *faster and faster*
- *just in time*
- *panic?*
- *move to the side of the avalanche and escape*
- *lucky to be alive*
- *If he hadn't escaped the avalanche…*
- *over and over again*
- *zoom in*
- *slow motion*

You could write a list like this and hold it in your hand. But for English language teachers, I would suggest that you also make it visible for everyone to see by displaying it on the board. Alternatively, write each phrase on an individual piece of paper and stick them around the classroom walls in the correct order. This will give students a very rough idea of where they are going in the story - at least from a language point of view - and is excellent for strengthening comprehension.

Make Eye Contact
Good eye contact is important for good communication. It allows us to monitor and develop an awareness of our audience.

It allows us to see who is paying attention and who is not. It also allows us to identify who seems confused or frustrated.

Move your eyes around the room and try to make contact with different students at different moments. Although you are telling the story to a room of people, there can be moments in which individuals think that you are speaking to them personally.

Give Students Space

The teacher's voice can be a dominating force! Sometimes, less is more. Slow down and use pauses to reduce the pace and density of your teacher talk. Silence doesn't have to be awkward and uncomfortable. Sometimes it is essential. It provides students with space to think and to formulate questions and answers. For English language learners, it also provides space to process language and hear sounds.

Manage a Digression

Digression can be an inevitable part of a group discussion. In order to get things back on track, make use of the phrases: *Anyway, where were we?* or *Yes, so let's get back to our story.* You can then invite students to recap the story so far or you can do it yourself.

Look Back

For English language teachers, whenever possible, remind students when and where they met a language item before. Perhaps a word appeared in a text, in a course book unit, or in another story. Or it may have come up during a class discussion. Information like this will allow students to make connections – an important part of the language learning process.

Provide a Strong Beginning and Ending

Begin and end your story confidently. My personal favorite lines are: *I want to tell you a story but first let me ask you a question,* and *And that's the end of the story. Or is it?*

Non-verbal Communicative Techniques

Gesture

With a bit of creativity, there are countless ways to reinforce meaning with hand, arm, and body movements. Here are some examples:

- "The Story of David and Matthew" (chapter 3): As you tell the story, you can mime all of these actions: *He puts his hand in his pocket, takes out a coin, and places it on the counter. Matthew takes the coin and gives a scratch card to David. David takes another coin out of his pocket and starts to scratch.*

- "Left on the Shelf" (chapter 4): *He was going one way* [point in one direction], *she was going the other* [point in the opposite direction].

- "Love and Chaos" (chapter 5): *It seems to communicate a contrast between love on one hand* [hold up your left hand] *and chaos on the other* [hold up your right hand].

Body Position

Like gesture, body position is another excellent way of reinforcing meaning. Here are some examples:

- "Splat!" (chapter 4): *Two young men are at work. They are sitting at a table* [gesture the shape of a table with your hand]: *Gavin is on the left* [stand on the left of the imaginary table] *and Daniel is on the right* [stand on the right of the imaginary table].

- "Zwier's New Toy" (chapter 4): As you tell this story, plan out an imaginary reconstruction of the canal. Make sure that students know where the edge is and where the centre is. The drone is going to land in the centre. You can also use gesture to reinforce where the water is: *up to his waist, up to his chest, up to his neck, up to his chin.*

Sound Effects

Look for possibilities for including your own sound effects. For example:

- "Pogo and the Mystery Object" (chapter 3): *Today Pogo is taking his afternoon siesta in the sun, when suddenly... THUD!* [bring down a fist on the palm of your hand].

- "OMG! WTH?" (chapter 4): *This big, round metal object. It whistles through the air* [point to the ceiling and bring your finger down slowly as you make a descending whistle sound].

- "Left on the Shelf" (chapter 4): *He popped* [pierce a sealed mouthful of air with your finger] *the question.*

Visual Support

Visual support could be any of the following:

- quick sketches on the board
- images obtained from an image search site
- the illustrations in this book

Here are some moments from stories that could require visual support:

- *"Lepus arcticus"* (chapter 1): Use a map to show students exactly where the story takes place - in the Kamchatka Peninsula, in northeast Russia.

- "Splat!" (chapter 4): If English language learners don't know what a watermelon is, the impact will be lost when you get to that part of the story. In this case, have a picture of a watermelon ready.

- "The Story of a Wannabe YouTuber and a Carolina Reaper" (chapter 4): If students are unable to guess what a California reaper is, show them an image. When they see it, they might be able to guess that it is the hottest chili pepper in the world.

Objects and Props
Whenever possible, complement a story with objects or props. This can be engaging for students. English language teachers can also refer to an object to teach its name. Some examples:

- "A World Champion" (chapter 1): Use real objects to teach the vocabulary: *the board, a wet sponge,* and *a piece of chalk.* Tell students that you are going to tell them a story which involves these things, called "A World Champion". Ask students to guess what happens in it.

- "Unusual Recipe" (chapter 2): If you are the kind of teacher who likes preparation (little joke there!), try to get hold of all of the objects that feature in this story (a Rubik's Cube, glitter, rubber bands, etc.). Before you do the activity, pass the objects around the class and ask everyone to think of three verbs that could be associated with each one. (For example, glitter could be associated with *sprinkle, sparkle,* and *decorate.*) The next day do the "Unusual Recipe" story. Students will see all of those objects in the video.

- "The Box" (chapter 3): Before you start the story, take a matchbox out of your pocket and place it on top of your desk for everyone to see. This will intrigue students. English language teachers can also teach the difference between *a box of matches* (full) and *a matchbox* (referring to the box alone).

The Board
This may seem obvious, but in my experience, many teachers feel that the board is off limits when telling a story. Of course, it is not. We can turn to it at any time - before, during, or after the storytelling - to present students with new English language items. After all, many learners claim that they need to see the language written down if they are to memorize it. We can also use the board to draw illustrations which complement the story. This was described in "Fun with an Electric Fence" (chapter 3).

Enhancing Comprehension

Grading your Language

When telling stories, asking questions, and conversing with your students, pay attention to the language choices that you make. Avoid using low-frequency (uncommon) words and phrases that your students will not know. And don't assume that students will understand obscure idioms or references to cultural ideas. This can be especially important for English language teachers and teachers of young learners.

Paraphrasing

If students don't understand a language item, find another way to express it. *In other words* is an excellent phrase to use for this purpose. For example, in "Left on the Shelf" (chapter 4) we could say: *He popped the question. In other words, he asked her to marry him. She said yes. They tied the knot. In other words, they got married.*

Repeating Key Words

Recapping parts of a story and repeating key lines are excellent devices for aiding comprehension. Repetition provides students with multiple opportunities to hear and process the text. For English language teachers, repetition also increases the possibility for students to notice language features in the story. Don't be afraid to go back over parts of the story two or even three times.

Using Catchphrases

Consider using catchphrases. These can be short phrases or sentences that you repeat throughout a story. For example, in "Jamie's All-Time Favourite TV Advertisement" (chapter 2), notice how many times I repeat the phrase *big fat hairy belly*. As well as creating a comical effect, catchphrases can be "sticky" and memorable. This can be good for English language learners.

In the case of *big fat hairy belly*, for example, the phrase illustrates some predictable features of language:

- order of adjectives (you wouldn't say ~~hairy big fat belly~~ or ~~fat hairy big belly~~)
- the fact that the stress usually falls on the noun (*belly*)

Using Dictation

During a standard dictation for English language learners, the activity follows a familiar pattern:

- The teacher reads aloud a short text (or a list of words, phrases, sentences, questions, etc.). Each line of the text is usually repeated two or three times.
- Students listen carefully and write down what they hear, word for word.
- Students get into pairs and compare what they have written.
- Finally, the teacher shows students the original text. Students compare it with their own versions and make corrections as necessary.

Dictation is an excellent language practice exercise. As well as requiring intensive listening, it is great for encouraging students to notice features such as sound-spelling relationships, collocation, and grammatical structures. It can also have an instantly calming effect on the most active group of students. Dictation could be used in any of the following ways:

- Dictate an entire story text. This would be practical for some of the shorter texts such as "Eagle Eyes" (chapter 1), "Terrified" (chapter 2), "Splat!" (chapter 4), or "A Gentle Giant?" (chapter 5).
- Before telling a story, dictate a list of isolated story items (a technique explained in chapter 4).
- For English language learners, dictate excerpts from a story that illustrate a grammar point. For example, before or after

telling the story of *"Lepus arcticus"* (chapter 1) you could dictate the conditional structure: *If I hadn't escaped the avalanche, I wouldn't have survived.*

Translating Words and Phrases

For English language teachers who have knowledge of their students' language(s), two fundamental questions are:

- *How do/would/could you say that in English?*
- *How do/would/could you say that in your language?*

You can ask these questions at any time when you need to clarify the meaning of a word or phrase in a story. I also like to make use of these questions whenever a dialogue takes place in the story. For example, when using "The Box" (chapter 3) with Spanish-speaking students, I would ask:

- *Aleksander takes off his glasses, looks directly at Adam and says: "No la abras."* **How do you say that in English?**
- *Adam replies: "¿Por qué no?"* **How do you say that in English?**
- *Aleksander replies: "Because you might regret it."* **How could you say that in Spanish?**

Encouraging Student Involvement

Modelling Actions

Invite students to gesture actions in a story as they hear it. For example, in "A World Champion" (chapter 1) you could model actions for any of the following and ask students to join in:

- *The camcorder is turned on and pointed at Alex.*
- *The image is shaky.*
- *"I'm going to tell you the story", says Alex as he cleans the board in preparation with a wet sponge.*
- *He warms up by doing a special exercise with his right arm.*

- *The board is still wet. Alex attempts to make it dry faster by flapping his hands at it comically.*
- *Alex picks up a piece of chalk.*
- *He takes a deep breath and stands tall beside the board.*
- *The audience applauds.*

Pretending to Forget Words

At times, it can be fun and effective to pretend that you can't remember a word. Provide students with information about it and ask if they can help. It doesn't matter if they know that you are fooling around. For example, you could start "Pogo and the Mystery Object" (chapter 3) by saying:

So let me tell about Pogo. If I had to describe him, I would say that he is... [pause]. What's that word – it's an adjective that means that you don't like working? You would prefer to spend time in bed (answer: lazy). Also, he spends a lot of time thinking about food and he eats too much [pause] (answer: greedy). And what's that adjective that you would use to describe a child that asks lots of questions? (answer: curious). So yes. Pogo is lazy, greedy, and curious.

Of course, there is other information that we can supply in addition or instead of definitions:

- *It rhymes with...*
- *It begins with the letter...*
- *It has [x] number of syllables...*
- *It is the opposite of...*
- *It has a meaning which is similar to...*

Encouraging Lip-Reading

This can be a good technique for English language teachers. When recapping a story, silently mouth a sentence or phrase that students have already heard. Ask them to read your lips and recall the sentence or phrase.

Using Acronyms/Abbreviations

This approach is particularly useful for English language teachers. After hearing a story, give students the first letters to the words in a phrase or sentence and ask them to guess or recall what the whole words are. For example, once students have heard "Splat!" two or three times (chapter 4), write the following acronyms/abbreviations on the board but don't give away the answers for each, which are on the right.

- *TYMAAW*   *two young men are at work*
- *SAAT*   *sitting at a table*
- *GIOTL*   *Gavin is on the left*
- *DIOTR*   *Daniel is on the right*
- *SOEO*   *sitting opposite each other*
- *ETS*   *eyes tightly shut*
- *ATT*   *above the table*
- *ITSBT*   *in the space between them*

Ask students to work out the full phrases, which are rich in prepositions.

Using a Hands-Up Poll

This is a very useful device for keeping students involved. Quite simply, ask for a show of hands whenever students are faced with a decision to make. For example, in "Unusual Recipe" (chapter 2), ask: *Okay, so who thinks that "pintoes tots" is butter? Put up your hands. And who thinks that it is cream? Put up your hands...*

Creating Chants

Some stories have structures or passages which are suitable for a "call and response" chant. For example, "Why Are You Lying on the Pavement?" (chapter 2) contains a repetitive element which would work for this approach:

Teacher: *What's going on here?*

Students: *What's going on here?*

Teacher: *Why is this man lying in the middle of the pavement?*
Students: *Why is this man lying in the middle of the pavement?*
Teacher: *What's wrong with him?*
Students: *What's wrong with him?*
Teacher: *Has he been drinking?*
Students: *Has he been drinking?*
Teacher: *Has he fallen?*
Students: *Has he fallen?*
Teacher: *Is he injured?*
Students: *Is he injured?*
Teacher: *Is he mad?*
Students: *Is he mad?*

Asking a Question but Forbidding an Answer

This may sound like a strange idea, but it can be an alternative to the "hands up who knows the answer" approach, which can be a bit pointless sometimes. Ask a question and immediately put your finger to your lips. This should indicate that you do not want students to shout out their answers. After a few moments of silence, nominate a student and ask that student to give the answer.

The idea is that this requires that everyone in the class thinks about the question and prepares an answer to give. An alternative approach is to ask everyone to write down their ideas on pieces of paper or on mini hand-held white boards.

Using Different Sides of the Classroom

Ask students to move to one side of the room or another, according to whether they agree or disagree with an idea. From here, ask students from different sides of the room to pair up and discuss their differences of opinion. For example, in "A Man With a Passion" in chapter 5, you could ask students to choose whether or not they think the video stereotypes people with disabilities.

Creating Pyramid Discussions

Ask students to get into pairs to discuss an issue. Once they have done this, ask different pairs to get together to form groups of four. After comparing ideas, groups of four can combine to form groups of eight, and so on. Eventually, the whole class will be together in a single group. This can be a good way of asking the class to come to a consensus about something. For example, in "Why Are You Lying on the Pavement?" in chapter 2, the following question could be used to set up a pyramid discussion: *So if you found someone lying on the pavement, what would you do? Would you help or not? What would it depend on?*

Using "Think, Pair, Share"

This is a simple and effective way for students to support each other's comprehension. In response to a question, give students some space to process it (think), turn to a partner (pair), and discuss their answers (share). After they share their ideas with each other, you can then invite students to share them with the rest of the class.

Using Question Tokens

In situations when students may be reluctant to interact and ask questions (with shy groups, for example), you can make use of question tokens. These can be pieces of card, bottle tops, buttons, plastic coins, etc. When a student asks a question, he or she has to give the question token back to you. Everyone in the class must spend his or her token before you get to the end of the story.

Using Audio Only

This is a great way to get students making predictions before they hear a video-based story. Play the video so that students can hear it but not see it. Then ask them to say what they hear (or think they hear) and guess what's happening. After this, you can move onto the story. This would work for any of the following videos:

- "Sneezing Baby Panda" in the introduction: Before you tell the story "Something Unexpected", play the video audio and ask students to guess what is going on.

- "Mr. W" in chapter 1: After you tell the story "Always Misunderstood", play the video audio and ask students to make a list of everything that they hear.

- "Beans" in chapter 2: After students guess about the genre of the video, let them hear the audio. This may reinforce their ideas or force them to reconsider.

- "Electric Fence Experiment Ends as Expected" in chapter 3: Before you tell the story "Fun with an Electric Fence", play the video audio and ask students to guess where the video was shot, who is in it, and what they are doing.

- "The Real Blind Man Honesty Test" in chapter 5: For English language teachers, let your learners hear the video before they see it, and ask them to make a note of key words and phrases that they hear.

Appendix 4:
Video Cameras in the Students' Hands

Throughout this book, there are many suggestions for students to create their own stories. Traditionally, students might hand in written assignments or tell their stories live in class. In the videoblogging spirit, we can also give students the option to capture their storytelling performances on talking head videos. After all, spoken words on video are nothing more than an alternative to written words on paper - a different medium.

This approach could be applied to any of the "Students as Storytellers" or "Students as Videotellers" ideas, as well as many of the suggested follow-up tasks. These include:

- Describe an animal video. ("Something Unexpected" in the introduction)
- Create a horror story based on the life and death of a food item or everyday object. ("Halloween Horror Story" in chapter 1)
- Tell the story from the hare's point of view (*"Lepus arcticus"* in chapter 1)
- Describe an advertisement that you like. ("Jamie's All-Time Favourite TV Advertisement" in chapter 2)
- Describe your unusual recipe. ("Unusual Recipe" in chapter 2)
- Retell a story and predict the ending. ("The Box" in chapter 3)
- Describe a video and interpret it. ("The Woman with the Big Heart" in chapter 4)
- Create a story based on a nature documentary. ("A Story of Real Estate and Death" in chapter 4)
- Text reconstruction or dictogloss activities. ("A Killer Product" in chapter 4)
- Describe how you would bring this video to life. ("OMG! WTH?" in chapter 4)

All of my experience tells me that results are generally better if students have total control of the technology. So, as teachers, we can set up the tasks and provide technical advice. But students should create their own videos in their own time, in their own homes, using their own devices (mobile phones, tablet computers, or video cameras).

There are also suggestions in this book for collaborative film-making tasks (see "Left on the Shelf" in chapter 4, for example).

For teachers who are interested in setting up video-creation tasks, there are questions to ask, issues to consider, and problems to overcome. This appendix shares a few of my thoughts about these.

Parental Permission

Before asking young students to create videos, it is absolutely essential to have authorization from the school and to get parental permission. Check school policy and find out what procedures are in place and what support is available.

The standard way to obtain permission is by sending a letter or email to parents in which you specifically outline your intentions, expectations of students, and outcomes. Explain how and why you intend to incorporate video cameras into your lessons. Parents will then have to return the letters or emails with their signatures of consent.

It is important to be as specific as possible about your intentions. For example, if you would like students to share their videos online, parents must know about this. How do you intend students to share their videos? What site do you recommend? And once a video is online, what do you intend to do with it? There are various ways to inform parents and "sell" your idea:

- Show an example: If possible, try to refer parents to a good example of a student-created video. This is one of the best ways of making your intentions clear.

- Discuss content ownership: Stress that the students will be making use of their own devices for filming. This means that they will retain ownership of the digital content.

- Involve parents: Invite parents to get involved and monitor their child's work. They should make sure that they are happy with it before it is submitted or shared.

- Invite parents to control the content: If you want students to share their videos online, mention to parents that they can oversee the process. They can upload the video on a site of their own choice (Vimeo or YouTube, for example). And since they will upload it to their own channel or account, they will be able to select the suitable privacy option (discussed below).

In this way, parents will also have freedom to remove their child's video whenever they like.

Choice of Medium

Not everyone enjoys appearing on camera. And some people express themselves better through the written word. Offer your students a choice of medium. Tell them that they can either submit a talking head video or a written assignment. Alternatively, they could submit their stories as audio files rather than video files.

Sharing

Once students have created a video file, they will have to make it available to you and, preferably, their classmates as well. All of the following are options:

- Using memory sticks: This approach is simple but can leave you with a lot of work as you sort through the sticks and files. The other disadvantage is that, when handed in on memory sticks, video files are not accessible to other students. And remember — of course — that memory sticks can spread computer viruses.

- Playing directly from a student's device: You can connect a student's smartphone or tablet computer directly to a classroom projector or TV screen. This will allow the whole class to view the student's video without the need for online sharing. However, in order to do this, you will need the appropriate adaptor or adaptors.

- Cloud sharing (e.g. Dropbox and Google Drive): This can be a good way of making video files available to everyone through a shared folder (see the accompanying website).

- Using video-sharing sites (e.g. YouTube and Vimeo): Students can upload a video on their own channel or account, and share the link in a communal space such as a VLE (virtual learning environment) or on an Edmodo, Padlet, or Pinterest page (see the accompanying website). Although this is an attractive option, privacy is a key issue, as I next describe.

Privacy and Online Safety

If students or students' parents are going to upload videos onto video-sharing sites, they should be sure to select the best privacy options. For example, Vimeo allows users to protect their videos with passwords. And YouTube allows users to upload their videos as unlisted. This means that they cannot be found via a search of the site.

Students should also be aware of potential dangers associated with online video, such as bullying and online hate. Speak with your students and discuss these issues. Make sure that they are fully aware of the dangers. Remind them that they have to be responsible. And make it absolutely clear that any form of online bullying between classmates – in or out of the classroom – will not be tolerated.

Technical Support for Filmmaking

In some cases, students may be advanced users of video tools. But we can't assume that. Time and time again, I have found that my own students require some basic technical support. Make sure that students understand that, when creating a talking head video, they should do the following:

- Choose a quiet location, away from background noise (other people speaking, traffic, etc.).
- Make sure that there is suitable lighting. The light source should be in front of the face – not behind it.
- Frame the shot well. Students should get close to the camera and fill the frame. Eyes should be positioned approximately two thirds of the way up the screen.
- Avoid vertical videos. Students should position the camera so that it is horizontal.

- Use a mobile phone stand, tripod, or selfie stick if possible.
- Speak loudly and clearly.

In some cases, students may want to film each other. When doing so, they should make sure not to hold a finger against the microphone or camera lens. Also, they should avoid moving the camera around needlessly or standing too far away from their subject.

Editing

A little bit of editing can make all the difference. A video editing tool such as Windows Movie Maker (PC) or iMovie (Apple) can be used to increase audio levels, trim videos, remove unwanted parts of videos, and add subtitles and credits.

For more advanced projects - collaborative films, for example - students can use video editing tools to put different shots into sequence.

Video Models

If possible, when setting a video task, show students a good example of what they are expected to produce. This model could be a video created by another student (with that student's permission, of course). Use the video to draw students' attention to good practice and technical aspects:

- good lighting
- good volume levels
- well-framed shots
- good eye contact with the camera
- editing techniques
- good communication

Time Limits

In my experience, students tend to submit videos that are too long. This will often result from insufficient planning or no editing. Give students a time limit. Tell them that they have to create a video that is no longer than one minute, for example.

Location and Aesthetics

The classroom is not an ideal place for video creation. When more than one person is creating a video, the result can be a noisy environment. In addition, many schools ban mobile phones from the classroom. But this is not a problem. Video production tasks work much better outside the classroom and make good homework assignments. This allows students to take their time, choose relevant locations, choose what they want to wear, and make themselves look good for the camera. They can also choose to use props, if necessary.

Scripting

There are very few situations in which people go in front of video cameras without having an idea of what they are going to say. When planning a video, scripting is the norm.

However, this issue presents us with some considerations. When creating a talking head video, for example, eyes are expected to be directed to the camera lens. But if students are using notes, the result will so often be "eyes down" reading. This does not lend itself to a good video.

When creating collaborative films, students can learn their lines by heart. But when creating talking head videos, it is not fair to demand this memorization. One possibility is to introduce students to a popular editing technique called "jump cuts", which uses the following steps:

- The student breaks a prepared script into smaller, memorable chunks.
- The student commits these chunks to short-term memory – one at a time – and communicates them "eyes up" to the camera.
- During this time, the camera records continuously.

- Later, at the editing stage, the student uses *snip* and *delete* functions to remove all of the redundant pieces of video. This creates a series of jump cuts.
- The result is a video in which all of the individual chunks come together. This creates the illusion of continuity.

I have created an instructional video to demonstrate this (see the accompanying website).

Finally, for talking head videos, a confident introduction and a solid finish can really contribute to the product. Ask students to pay particular attention to how they are going to start and end a video. What are the very first and very last things that they are going to say?

Feedback

Many of the suggested student tasks in this book include ideas for making stories interactive. For example, describe a funny animal video that you like but don't say what the animal is. Or describe an advertisement that you like but don't say what the product is.

Tasks like these work best if students can access each other's videos outside class. This will allow them to watch videos, make guesses (e.g. What is the mystery product or animal?), and leave comments.

We can also ask students to give feedback on each other's videos. One good way to encourage peer-to-peer feedback is to create a feedback rubric. This is a form which is divided into the different areas that we want to draw attention to. These could include any or all of the following:

- quality of audio
- length of video
- eye contact
- story structure
- language choices

- pronunciation
- grammatical accuracy
- fluency
- editing
- how well the student has fulfilled the task overall

For each video that they watch, students should write a comment for each of these things. Rubrics are also good for self-evaluation and reflection.

There are other possibilities. With the storyteller's consent, you can play a video on the big screen for whole-class viewing and feedback. English language teachers can make use of the pause button to stop a video and elicit feedback and/or draw attention to aspects of effective use of language.

Appendix 5:
Video Cameras in the Teacher's Hands

Many of the activities in this book can be enhanced with video content of your own. We can make use of our mobile phones or tablet computers to create quick talking head videos to use in the classroom. Here are some ideas:

Filming Yourself
Sometimes it can be difficult to get your students' attention. Whether we are giving instructions, demonstrating a task, explaining an idea or telling a story, we can never be sure who is listening and who is not.

If you really want to get your message heard, try something new: Before going into the classroom, address your students in a short talking head video. And when you go into class, connect your device to a projector and play the video on the big screen for everyone to see.

This is not something that I do every day. But when I do, it seems to intrigue students and get their attention instantly. Even stranger is this: immediately after seeing the video, students will often be happy to watch it a second time.

In the introduction and chapter 1, there is a suggested task that asks students to go online and find an animal video that they like. They should then describe the video without saying what the animal is. (They can give it a human name if they like.) Here is a transcript of a video that I made myself to model the task:

Story: "Doris and Raspberries"

I want to tell you about a video on YouTube

And it involves a mystery animal, and I'm going to call her Doris

And in this video Doris is enjoying some raspberries

And they look great

They look delicious – really juicy

And Doris is really enjoying these raspberries

And the funny thing about this video is that

As she eats the raspberries, her lips get bright red

And it looks like she's wearing lipstick

Bright red lipstick all around her mouth

And she's got no idea

She's just an animal

So it probably makes no difference to her anyway

But her lips are getting bright red

She looks like an aristocratic woman

With bright red lips

It makes me laugh

Anyway that's Doris and the raspberries

And you've got to try and guess what kind of animal Doris is

You can see this video on my YouTube channel – see the accompanying website.

In the classroom, there are at least three things that I can do with a video like this:

- Model the task: Rather than telling students what they have to do, this video allows me to show them.

- Model the product: I can draw attention to technical aspects of the video (e.g. clear audio and good lighting) as well as aspects of communication (e.g. the fact that I communicate "eyes up" to the camera). Students should aim for these things when they create their own videos.

- Model the language: For English language learners, I can refer to features of my spoken language that I want them to use (e.g. the fact that I use present narrative tenses to describe Doris's actions). I can also draw attention to my opening and closing lines, and ask students to incorporate these into their own videos.

Filming Friends

In one of the stories in this book, students have to speculate about why a well-dressed, fully conscious man is lying in the middle of the pavement ("Why Are You Lying on the Pavement?" in chapter 2). I put this question to some friends and family members and filmed their responses with my mobile phone. Here are some of the answers that I got:

- *"I think the man is lying on top of a bomb, and if he gets up, the bomb will detonate."* (my brother's idea)
- *"I think that the man has ripped his trousers and he doesn't want to get up because he's embarrassed."* (my friend Jono's idea)
- *"I think that he saw a large value bank note and it was too obvious to pick it up so he lay down on top of it."* (my mum's idea)

You can see this video on my YouTube channel – see the accompanying website. It seems that there are lots of possibilities here. But what about your students? Will their answers be as creative as this? In my experience, students often have good ideas but feel shy or awkward about sharing them.

In cases like this, I can show students the video that I made and introduce them to my brother, my mum, and my friend Jono. Now the task is different – students have to listen to the three answers and decide which one they like the best. This will require students to evaluate and reject, or build on the ideas that they hear. And this process in itself can sometimes provide the spark for the discussion that you wanted.

Other Possibilities

I have subjected many friends to the speaking tasks in this book and captured their responses on camera. For example, in one of my videos, you can hear James referring to some isolated story items to predict what happens in the story "Zwier's New Toy" (chapter 4):

Well, I think that the man in question has bought a DJI Phantom. It's new to him and he's very enthusiastic – he's desperate to try it. And even though it's December and it's cold and it isn't the perfect conditions for flying drones, he decides that he's going to do it anyway. But while he's flying it, he gets distracted and he ends up walking into a canal filled with ice-cold water. Now of course, when he does that, he loses control of the drone and the drone, being intelligent, makes an automatic landing and thus saves the man a lot of money. It doesn't crash to the ground as you would expect. It lands on its own and even though he's wet and he's cold, his drone is okay.

You can see this video on my YouTube channel – see the accompanying website.

In the classroom, a video like this can be a valuable piece of material. Before students do the task themselves, I can use the video for any or all of the following:

- To model the task: No matter how clear we try to make our instructions, there will always be some students who are unsure about what they have to do. A video like this allows us to demonstrate the task (i.e. to predict what happens in the story from the isolated story items).

- To spark imaginations: As already mentioned, students can respond to the content of the video. In this case, they can guess whether or not James's prediction is correct. Then tell students that he does not predict correctly and invite them to try it for themselves.

- To model the language: English language teachers can draw attention to words and phrases that James uses (*to fly a drone, to get distracted, to end up walking into a canal, to lose control of the drone, to make an automatic landing*, etc.). When students do the task, they can then use these words and phrases themselves if they wish to do so.

Transcripts and Adapted Transcripts

In chapter 1, we looked at possibilities for using and adapting video transcripts. This strategy could be particularly useful for

English language teachers. The following is an adapted transcript of a video which features a number of colleagues from my teaching institute. I made the video to introduce the "Worst Best Man" activity in chapter 3.

English language learners have to predict the missing verbs in the transcript before watching the video:

Jamie: *Can you think of something that could go wrong at a wedding?*

Ali: *The bride doesn't _____ up.*

Anna: *Someone _____ on the wedding cake.*

Hanna: *The bride _____ over her dress on the way to the altar in the church.*

María: *The groom _____ drunk.*

James: *Someone else _____ on the same day and takes all the attention away from the bride and groom.*

Chris: *Somebody gets too drunk and it _____ in a massive fight.*

Tom: *The best man _____ the rings.*

Ria: *They _____ out that the bride and the best man have been having an affair.*

You can see this video on my YouTube channel – see the accompanying website. Answers are *turn, falls, trips, gets, proposes, ends, forgets, find.*

Making Your Own Videos

One thing that fascinates human beings is other human beings. A video that introduces your students to your own friends, colleagues, and family members can be a powerful teaching resource. It can create a personal and memorable experience. Here are some tips:

- Make use of the staff room: If you are a last-minute person like me, the staff room can be a great place to film responses from other teachers. Explain to your colleagues what you intend to do with the video. Tell them that if they ever want to do the same, you will be happy to pay back the favour and appear in one of their videos.

- Give people time to prepare: After setting the task, give the person enough time to formulate an answer. This could be anything from a few seconds to a few minutes.
- Keep it short: Before filming, tell the person that you are looking for something short and concise.
- Do retakes: Let the person see the video and make sure that he or she is happy with it. If not, you can shoot it again.
- Ask the person to speak loudly and clearly.
- Confirm permission and privacy: Make sure you tell the person what you want to do with the video. And if he or she is under eighteen, you will need parental permission.
- Personalize it: For friends and family members, you could ask them to say hello to your students or give them a personal message.

Technical Tips

Mobile devices are excellent for creating videos like this. Here are some technical tips:

- Choose a quiet location with good lighting.
- Hold your device so that it is horizontal (in landscape format) and avoid vertical videos.
- Get close to the speaker. The frame should be filled with his or her head and shoulders. Eyes should be positioned approximately two thirds of the way up the screen.
- Make sure that you do not put your finger over the microphone or camera lens.
- Keep the video camera as still as possible. Fix it on the person and do not move it around needlessly.
- Two of the videos that I have referred to in this appendix are montage videos - they consist of multiple clips of different people. You can use video editors to create videos like this.

Appendix 6: English Language Teachers

In this appendix, I would like to share some additional ideas and support for English language teachers.

Language Learner Levels

As a basic guide, I have graded each story in this book according to the levels described by *The Common European Framework of Reference for Languages* (CEFR). You can see this information in the table below. The levels are as follows:

A2 - elementary
B1 - intermediate
B2 - upper intermediate
C1 - advanced

Please note that these levels refer only to the language in the story texts. In some cases, the tasks and activities that I have suggested will be more challenging.

Planning for Comprehension

When preparing a story for language learners, it is important to anticipate words and phrases in the text that (a) students may be unfamiliar with and (b) are essential for comprehension. There is an important difference here. In some cases, students will be able to comprehend a story even if they don't know or can't identify every word that they hear. But in other cases, there are certain words, phrases, and ideas that are essential for comprehension. For example, in "A Story of Real Estate and Death" (chapter 4), students must understand the phrase *the tide is out* or else the story will make no sense.

The table below lists the stories and their CEFR grades. It also offers a list of suggestions for words and phrases that you may have to introduce to students before telling the stories.

STORY TITLES	GRADE	WORDS AND PHRASES
Introduction		
"Something Unexpected"	A2	Something unexpected (happens)
Chapter 1		
"Feeding Time"	B1	Watermelon; a grape; a zookeeper
"Always Misunderstood"	B1	Misunderstood (to misunderstand someone); to get on someone's nerves; intense (to describe a person); to come on too strong
"Halloween Horror Story"	B1	Cruel; dragging; to fade in the distance; to feel dizzy; ribbons; to pray
"Eagle Eyes"	B1	Eyesight; contact lenses; binoculars; to have eagle eyes (the ability to see things in the distance); to spot (to see)
"An Act of True Love"	B2	To be obsessed with something or someone; a hailstone; a melon; a grape; to flap your arms and legs; furious movements
"A Tale of Two Ryans"	B1	A close-up shot of a bowl of cornflakes; a spoonful of cereal; to sneak in; the mainstream media; a salute (a gesture of respect)
"A World Champion"	B1	Shaky (not stable); a sponge; to flap your hands comically (in a funny way)
"*Lepus arcticus*"	B1	An avalanche; to panic; to play (a video) in slow motion; to zoom in (on something); a hare

STORY TITLES	GRADE	WORDS AND PHRASES
Chapter 2		
"An Audition"	B1	(To go for) an audition; a resumé; a receptionist; to monkey around (similar to mess around – to behave in a silly way); the (audition) venue
"Jamie's All-Time Favourite TV Advertisement"	A2	A big fat hairy belly
"On the Moon"	B2	In the foreground; in the background; an astronaut; Mission Control (the place on Earth from which they control the space mission); a crater; a monster; trembling; terrified; terrifying; a fart; a slogan
"Why Are You Lying on the Pavement?"	A2	Pavement (sidewalk); a pedestrian
"Terrified"	A2	A corridor; haunted; a dressing gown; terrified; terrifying
"Lambs to the Slaughter"	B1	Lambs to the slaughter; cattle; the slaughterhouse; unsure; uneasy; begging eyes; the cargo
"Mystery Crop"	B1	A crop; a harvest; to drain; a mild winter
"Unusual Recipe"	B2	A handful; a spoonful; a clove (of garlic); a colander; ripe; to chop; to grate; to drain; to simmer; to sweeten; to squash; to stir

STORY TITLES	GRADE	WORDS AND PHRASES
"Catch of the Day"	C1	Catch of the day; crew members; to scrub the decks; the radar system; a harpoon; a shoal; to dock; a trader; processed and homogenized; preservatives; flavour enhancers; bulking agent; batches; a conveyor belt; a miniature replica
"Predator and Prey"		Predator and prey; a piece of footage; grassy plains (of Botswana); weeds; safety in numbers; the camera pans; a herd; the occasional twitch; to creep; to show signs of panic and restlessness; to disperse; to single out; to feast greedily on a carcass
Chapter 3		
"An Embarrassing Phone Call"	A2	A pet hate (a trivial thing that you find particularly annoying); a class policy; the loudspeaker; pregnancy; positive test results; counselling; to apologize
"The Story of David and Matthew"	A2	A creature of habit; a scratch card; a shopkeeper; to greet; the (shop) counter; to tear something in half
"Can't Hug Every Cat"	B1	Online dating; to register with a dating site; social media; a viral video; internet hate; to subscribe to a YouTube channel; to upload a video; to delete a video; to hug; to have an obsession; to have an addiction; an online celebrity; the dam bursts; flooded; to feel sorry for someone; paths crossed; death threats

STORY TITLES	GRADE	WORDS AND PHRASES
"A Man, a Woman, a Vase"	A2	A vase; to accuse someone of (doing) something
"The Box"	B1	A matchbox; a cellmate; to greet; a miniature model replica; to regret
"Pogo and the Mystery Object"	B1	A creature of habit; to do a parachute jump; turbulence
"Worst Best Man"	B1	A (priest's) gown
"Electric Fence Experiment Ends as Expected"	B1	An electric fence; an electric shock; an electric current; a wire; the earth
Chapter 4		
"Speechless"	A2	A court (various meanings); speechless (in shock)
"The Story of a Wannabe YouTuber and a Carolina Reaper"	A2	A YouTube channel; subscribers; to upload; the national and international media
"A Story of Real Estate and Death"	B2	Real estate; a risky acquisition; the housing market; fierce competition; the previous owner; shallow water; property buyers; a secure home; ready for release; the tide is out
"Zwier's New Toy"	B1	A canal; a drone; a safety feature; GPS (Global Positioning System); waist
"A Killer Product"	B2	To run a business; to pursue a career; an outsider; to see potential in someone; to become obsessed with something; a montage (a video that consists of a series of short related clips); a crowdfunding campaign; entrepreneurialism

STORY TITLES	GRADE	WORDS AND PHRASES
"Splat!"	B1	Watermelon; red flesh; green shell; drops of juice
"The Woman with the Big Heart"	B1	Strangers; without discrimination; a frown; a burden
"OMG! WTH?"	B1	Earpieces; a crumpled bonnet (hood); a satellite; to whistle through the air
"Left on the Shelf"	B1	Left on the shelf; love at first sight; made for each other; meant to be; against the odds (very unlikely); to pop the question (to propose to someone); to tie the knot (to get married); to go from strength to strength; beyond your control; against your will; to be forced apart; to go your separate ways
Chapter 5		
"A Gentle Giant?"	B1	A gentle giant; to be fooled; a demon; fiery; to hiss; to roar
"A Man with a Passion"	B1	To have a passion; recreational; an adrenaline rush; the skatepark (the place where skateboarders practise); a ramp; protective gear
"I Love Watermelon"	B1	LGBT (lesbian, gay, bisexual, and transgender); watermelon
"The Kuleshov Effect"	B1	A rock star; a town; a stage; a legendary singer; a traditional craft; video editing; to resurrect; arrogant; mocked (if you mock someone, you laugh at them and make them look stupid); the grave (place where a dead person is buried)

STORY TITLES	GRADE	WORDS AND PHRASES
"Captain Disillusion Versus the Tumba Ping Pong Show"	B2	A performing arts group; table tennis bats (or paddles); incredible skill; ping pong balls; darts; to spin through the air; to stick into; a pineapple; visual effects; rational thought; to expose a hoax; circular saw blades; a coconut; in the background; a hammer; in agony; revenge
"Honesty Test"	B1	Blind; to approach people; honesty; a social experiment; current affairs
"Love and Chaos"	B1	Chaos; kissing passionately; protesters; riot police; strangers in the crowd; overcome with mutual attraction; to embrace; a demonstration; a slogan
"The Story Behind Sneezing Baby Panda"	B1	Panda; levitated in shock; panda breeding; habitats; a cub; an enclosure; nutritional cookies; to sneeze; to lean down; to comfort

After the Storytelling

Once you have seen the video that a story is based on (i.e. after the moment of comparison), there is often a natural desire to revisit the story. When you do this, you may notice new details that you didn't appreciate the first time around. In other words, the language of the story text can become more meaningful after you have seen the video.

English language teachers can take advantage of this natural desire to revisit the story. We can give out copies of the story text to our students and invite them to experience it again – this time with a new level of comprehension. When we do this, we can set tasks that encourage them to personalize the text and notice language features in it. Here are three ideas:

1. Ask students to use the story text to create fill-the-gap activities for each other.

2. Give students a fixed time limit (one minute, for example) to attempt to memorize a text. When the time is up, ask students to hide their texts. Then go over the story again and improvise a storytelling gap fill (see chapter 4).

3. Ask students to choose their ten favourite words, phrases, idioms, or structures from the text – pieces of language that they would like to remember and take away with them. Then ask them to share their choices and say why they selected them.

Appendix 7:
The "Sneezing Baby Panda" Experiment

In 2007, I set up a resource website for teachers that is now called Lessonstream. The website was a place for me to share my video-based lesson plans and teaching ideas. One of my first posts involved a simple prediction activity which was based around the "Sneezing Baby Panda" video. I accompanied it with a classroom video, in which I demonstrated the activity with a group of English language learners.

One day, a comment appeared on the post, which read as follows:

Hello Jamie. Thanks for this lesson plan. My students and I enjoyed it. Just one thing: Why did you decide to teach your English learners the phrase "get a fright"? Would you really say that? It just doesn't seem natural to me.

This surprised me a lot. I felt certain that the most natural way to describe the event in the video is with the words *The baby panda sneezes and the mother panda gets a fright.* I couldn't think of a better way to express it. What was the problem here?

I looked for reassurance by asking other teachers and friends how they would describe the event. And unfortunately for me, most of them agreed with the commenter – that "get a fright" is not a phrase that they would use to describe the mother panda's reaction and probably not something that they would want to teach students with a pre-intermediate level of English.

I wanted to investigate this a bit further so, in order to do so, I set up a little experiment. I started to chase friends, students, family members, colleagues, and complete strangers. For each person, I did the following:

1. I showed them the "Sneezing Baby Panda" video.

2. I asked them to describe what they had just seen – in their own words – from start to finish.

3. I filmed their response.

Many of the resulting videos can be seen on my YouTube channel (the accompanying website). My experiment confirmed that the commenter on my website was right. In order to describe the mother panda's reaction, very few people used the phrase "get a fright". Here are some of the transcribed responses:

"… and the mother jumps. I didn't know animals could do that. I suppose it's a bit like can animals dream?"
"… and the mother freaks out."
"… and the mother gets frightened and then it's all over."
"… and momma panda nearly chokes on her bamboo."
"… and the mother panda was surprised."
"When the baby sneezed, the mother was shocked. She jumped."
"The smallest panda in the world just sneezes all of a sudden and scares the hell out of his giant mummy."
"Suddenly, the baby panda sneezes and she gives the mother a big panic and she just jumps, and it's really funny."

"*The tiny baby does a sneeze and this large panda, you know, just sort of like freaks out.*"

"*And then the little baby panda sneezes and [the mother panda] she's really, really shocked and just sort of jumps out of her skin - if a panda could jump out of its skin.*"

"*Suddenly, after a while, the baby panda shudders and sneezes and makes a very, very high-pitched noise, upon which the mother panda freaks out and seems to literally to jump off the ground into the air.*"

"*And the reaction of the big panda was immediately to lean forward and wonder - I suppose - what it was all about, and jumped. I suppose it was just a motherly reaction.*"

So what did I learn from this experiment? Well, out of the forty people that took part, exactly four of them used the phrase "get a fright". They were my mother, my brother, my father, and my sister:

"The baby sneezes violently and the mother panda gets a fright and jumps." (my mother, Anne)

"All of a sudden, baby panda sneezes without any warning at all. Mummy panda gets a big fright." (my brother, Alastair)

"All of a sudden, the baby sneezes and the mummy panda gets a big, big fright. Throws her hands up." (my father, Jack)

"And then the baby panda - lying on the floor between the mummy panda's legs - sneezes, and the mummy panda gets a big fright, and jumps." (my sister, Susie)

It would appear that for my siblings and parents, the phrase "get a fright" is a natural choice for describing the reactions of the sneezing baby panda's mother. But outside of my "speech community", that seemed not to be the case. That was an important lesson for me, as an English language teacher.

But perhaps more importantly, the experiment would seem to reinforce the idea that we all experience and interpret the video in different ways. There is only one "Sneezing Baby Panda" but an infinite number of ways to describe it. Different people notice different details. They make different associations and they ask different questions. In order to communicate, they use their own words, language choices, metaphors, images, gestures, and storytelling devices. And eventually, the pandas take secondary importance to people in the videos - they exist only as reflections in the personalities that I captured on my own camera.

About the Author

THIS BOOK IS the result of one man's love for story telling, his passion for teaching, and his addiction to YouTube. Jamie Keddie is a teenager in his early forties who, for the last decade, has been curating online videos and creating stories around them.

Videotelling is Jamie's third book. As an established Oxford University Press author, he is the man behind *Images* (2009) and *Bringing Online Video into the Classroom* (2014).

Jamie started off with a degree in biochemistry from the University of Aberdeen in Scotland. Realizing that he actually wanted to be a musician, he spent most of his twenties studying jazz at Leeds College of Music, in Yorkshire, England. After that, he worked as a singer-piano player on ships, but nothing too glamorous.

After getting tendonitis in his arms, Jamie was forced into a career change. He went to live in Spain and started working as an English teacher.

Now, as a Barcelona-based educator and teacher trainer, Jamie has shared his ideas and insights with teachers in over forty different countries. He gives plenary talks at international conferences and delivers workshops for primary, secondary, and language teachers. He is the founder of *Lessonstream*, an online resource for teachers.

In 2009, Jamie won a prestigious British Council ELTon award for his work. Sponsored by Cambridge English, the ELTons are the only international awards to recognize and celebrate innovation in English language teaching.

For more stories and storytelling ideas, subscribe to Jamie's newsletter at: jamiekeddie.com

For bookings, please get in touch at: jamiekeddie.com

Acknowledgments

I would like to thank the following people for their invaluable help, support, input, and expertise: Philip Kerr, Paul Martin Lester, Chris Rose, Marga Homar, Danny Butcher, Alastair Keddie, Susie Keddie, Anne Keddie, Edward Bettison, Peter Cocking, Trena White, Megan Jones, Nicola Meldrum, Laura Edlund, Joanna Reid, Captain Disillusion aka Alan Melikdjanian, Daniel Barber, Nick Bilbrough, Ben Goldstein, Billie Haase, Laura Plotnek-Jones, Agata Rybicka, Beata Palińska, Erica Robbins, and — of course — all the great people who contributed to the 2015 crowdfunding campaign which allowed me to get this book published. Thank you all, you lovely people!

STORY TITLE	THE STORY IS ABOUT	
A Gentle Giant?	A hot air balloon	
A Killer Product	Flies and crowdfunding	
A Man with a Passion	A blind skater	
A Man, a Woman, a Vase	A conversation	
A Story of Real Estate and Death	Hermit crabs and snails	
A Tale of Two Ryans	Ryan Gosling who won't eat his cereal	
A World Champion	Circles and maths teachers	
Always Misunderstood	Mr. W (the Wind)	
An Act of True Love	Cars and hail stones	
An Audition	An orangutan selling Levis jeans	
An Embarrassing Phone Call	April Fool's Day	
Can't Hug Every Cat	Online dating and cats	
Captain Disillusion Versus the Tumba Ping Pong Show	Visual effects	
Catch of the Day / Predator and Prey	Animals and humans changing places	
Eagle Eyes	Elizabeth the eagle	
Feeding Time	Hippos and watermelon	
Fun with an Electric Fence	Foolish / fearless teenagers	
Halloween Horror Story	Pumpkins	
Honesty Test	A social experiment involving a blind man	
I Love Watermelon	Sexuality and identity	
Jamie's All-time Favourite TV Advert	A big fat hairy belly	
Lambs to the Slaughter	Meat production	

SUBJECT CONNECTIONS	PAGE
Art; film studies; media studies; music; science	187
Art; business studies; design and technology; ethics; media studies	154
Ethics; film studies; music	192
Film studies; music	104
Biology; business studies; science	141
Film studies; literature studies; media studies	33
Art; art history; mathematics	38
Design and technology; environmental studies; film studies; media studies; science	19
Science	29
Biology; environmental studies; media studies; science	52
Cultural studies; social studies	89
Business studies; media studies; psychology; social studies	97
Film studies; media studies	207
Art; ethics; film studies; media studies; psychology	81
Biology; media studies	27
Biology; science	16
Design and technology; physics; science	128
Cultural studies	24
Citizenship; ethics; media studies; psychology; social studies	214
Citizenship; media studies; psychology; social studies	197
Media studies	56
Art; ethics; social studies	70

STORY TITLE	THE STORY IS ABOUT …
Left on the Shelf	Milk cartons in love
Lepus articus	An avalanche and Arctic hares
Love and Chaos	A riot kiss
Mystery Crop	The BBC spaghetti tree hoax
OMG! WTH?	A satellite prank video
On the Moon	Astronauts, beans, and a fart
Pogo and the Mystery Object	A pig, a skydiver, and a video camera
Something Unexpected	The sneezing baby panda
Speechless	A marriage proposal fail
Splat!	A watermelon explosion
Terrified	"Gangnam Style" and *The Shining*
The Box	Prison
The Kuleshov Effect	Freddie Mercury and Kanye West
The Story Behind Sneezing Baby Panda	The sneezing baby panda
The Story of a Wannabe YouTuber and a Carolina Reaper	Chili peppers
The Story of David and Matthew	A blind man and a scratch card
The Woman with the Big Heart	Alone in the city
Unusual Recipe	Spaghetti and tomato sauce
Worst Best Man	A wedding fail
Why Are You Lying on the Pavement?	Lying on the pavement and curiosity
Zwier's New Toy	A drone

SUBJECT CONNECTIONS	PAGE
Citizenship; drama; environmental studies	179
Biology; geography; sports; tourism	42
Art; citizenship; history; law; media studies	222
Cultural studies; design and technology; food studies; media studies; modern history	74
Design and technology; ethics; film studies; media studies	171
Media studies; science	59
Design and technology; physics	117
Biology; psychology	4
Psychology; social studies	134
Business studies; film studies; media studies; physics; science	161
Film studies; media studies	67
Citizenship; film studies; psychology	111
Film studies; media studies; music	201
Biology; media studies; psychology	226
Ethics; geography; media studies; science	137
Ethics; mathematics; psychology; social studies	93
Citizenship; psychology	165
Cooking; film studies	78
Cultural studies; media studies; religious studies	122
Citizenship; drama; psychology; social studies	63
Design and technology; ethics; law; psychology	149